Ron & Lynne Fellowes

Now retired, Ron spent his working life as diesel mechanic. For more than 50 years, he has ridden and restored vintage, veteran and classic machines. In his younger days, he raced speedway sidecars; tried road, trials and beach racing, and later, motocross. Today he enjoys participating in vintage motorcycle events and is currently planning his next overseas adventure.

Lynne worked as a freelance journalist. In the 1980s she and Ron rode 200,000 kilometres from the top of the world to the bottom. For a number of years she was a regular magazine contributor, and an online-training-program administrator. Lynne and Ron have lived in several countries and have now made their home in Tasmania.

No Room
for
Watermelons

a man, his 1910 motorcycle and
an epic journey across the world

Ron & Lynne Fellowes

High Horse

Published by High Horse Books
info@highhorse.com.au
& oldblokeonabike.com

Direct sales: ronfellowes@gmail.com
http://oldblokeonabike.com

Trade distribution: Dennis Jones & Associates
Unit 1/10 Melrich Road, Bayswater
Victoria 3153, Australia
www.dennisjones.com.au

Typeset in 11.5/14 Bembo by High Horse Books

National Library of Australia
Cataloguing-in-Publication data:

Fellowes, Ron, author. Fellowes, Lynne, author.
No room for watermelons:
a man, his 1910 motorcycle and an epic journey across the world
Ron Fellowes

ISBN: 9780646931418 (paperback)

Subjects:
Fellowes, Ron–Travel.
Motorcyclists–Biography.
Motorcycle touring.

629.2275092

www.highhorse.com.au
http://oldblokeonabike.com

To Effie

Istanbul to Liege

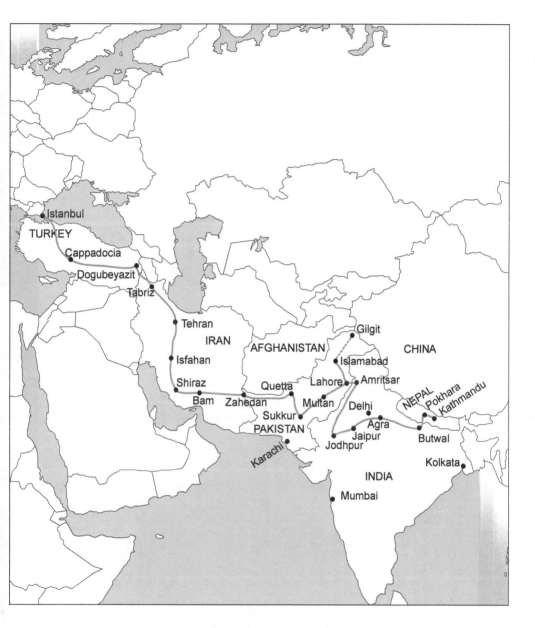

Kathmandu to Istanbul

Prelude

Some days go from bad to worse. They just do — sometimes without warning. Except this day was different. The gun should have been a clue.

I was squatting beside the old motorcycle, deep in thought, when a flash caught my eye. Instinctively I turned, just as the ringleader stepped towards me and put the shotgun to my head.

The other two boys fell silent.

Despite a gnawing sense of unease since their arrival, I hadn't anticipated this. After all, I had been on the road for months and had always felt comfortable among strangers.

I had been warned of the risks of travelling through Diyarbakir Province, where ethnic tensions make some areas unpredictable. I'd shrugged it off. People were often fearful of others, some even describing their neighbours as dangerous. Maybe, though, I should have listened to the gypsy, who had cautioned me earlier in the day.

This wasn't the first incident in recent months to rattle me. I'd been robbed, ridden through war zones and narrowly avoided terrorist attacks. I had to admit I often questioned why I was even attempting this crazy ride across the world. At times, the physical and mental challenge was almost too much to take. And, despite my apparent indifference to it, I knew the dangers.

So far, I'd been fortunate, but in that lonely field in the late afternoon, my luck looked like running out.

Was this how my journey was destined to end, and would I be making headlines for all the wrong reasons?

1

Easy Rider

A middle class upbringing in New Zealand after World War II taught me how to be resourceful, and that I could achieve anything I wanted — if I worked hard enough. From a young age, I earned money delivering the morning *Herald*. Customers tipped generously for my marksmanship: I could lob a rolled and bent newspaper onto their porch from the kerb 10 metres away.

On frosty winter mornings, I stuffed a few newspapers — hot off the press — down my shirt to ward off the cold. And, in what I thought was a stroke of genius, I filled the handlebars of my bicycle with boiling water and plugged each end with a cork. My hands stayed warm for at least 10 minutes, and two or three nine-penny meat pies staved off hunger until I made it home for breakfast. I worked at after-school jobs and on weekends I picked strawberries. During the holidays I apprenticed for an electrician. Despite my good work ethic, I was caned regularly at school and my most favourable school report read, 'Ronald is a born leader. It's just a shame he leads others in the wrong direction.'

At the age of 12, I rode on the back of a family friend's motorcycle, an experience that left me with a burn on my leg from a hot exhaust pipe and a fire in my belly to ride a machine of my own.

Within a year, I'd saved enough to buy my first motorcycle: a war-issue Harley Davidson, which I secretly stored at a neighbour's house. I spent every spare moment taking the engine apart and rebuilding it until I understood what made it tick. But it never saw the light of day; I couldn't afford a battery and wasn't even strong enough to kick it over. I gave the motorcycle back to its previous owner, and moved on to something more my size.

Too young to hold a licence, I made a go-kart from scrap and practiced honing my skills on a vacant piece of land. A scoria quarry nearby provided an excellent racetrack for my unbridled enthusiasm.

I persuaded a mate, whose parents were more well-heeled than mine, to let me test ride his Dot, then, later, his cool Norton Dominator. I was hooked on the exhilaration of riding, and dreamt of little else. But my father forbade me to own a motorcycle.

'They're dangerous, you'll bloody kill yourself,' he barked, rolling another cigarette. When Dad finally relented, he made one stipulation: my first bike could only have a maximum capacity of 175cc. A turquoise and cream N-Zeta scooter wasn't fast, nor did it match the image I had of myself as a boy racer, but it did have two wheels, and that was a start. Tearing up and down the streets with a gang of friends — whose motorcycles dripped oil and reverberated through the neighbourhood — pretty soon earned me a reputation as a hooligan.

Despite being sorely tested, my parents finally capitulated and agreed I could have a real motorcycle. Over the next couple of years, I acquired a side-valve Indian, a '56 Matchless, a DKW, a Velocette, a '34 and a '35 single Royal Enfield, and the bones of a highly prized Grey Flash Vincent.

The Vincent's tank and forks needed painting and I was confident I could achieve a baked enamel finish by doing the job myself. I rose early one morning, carefully heated an aerosol can of paint on the kitchen stove, and, when the paint was warm enough I gave the can a vigorous shake. BOOOOOM!

The arse blew clean out of the can, spraying grey paint all over my mother's newly decorated kitchen. The blast woke the family — in fact most of our neighbours. My ears rang like a smithy's anvil. Mum took one look at the chaos, burst into tears and ran back to the bedroom, leaving Dad and me to clean up the mess.

My Mum, bless her, soon forgave me and suggested I learn a trade. I had to agree. It made sense for me, as an avid collector of motorcycle junk, to become a mechanic. But my appetite for thrill-seeking continued unabated. Before long, I was trying my hand at trials riding, scrambles and beach and road racing. On one occasion, like a fool, I sped across Murewai beach with my right leg in plaster — the result of a recent crash. By the end of the day, the sodden cast had disintegrated. I wasn't game to go back to the hospital and admit to what I'd been up to, so I took the philosophical approach: if my broken ankle hadn't healed by now it probably never would.

My mate Grant 'Hickey' Innes and I excelled at falling off bikes and acting like clowns. While whistling and showing off to a group of schoolgirls one day, Grant spun the back wheel of his 500cc BSA and the two of us flew over the handlebars, landing in an embarrassing heap in front of the girls. They fell about laughing at our display of machismo, and laughed even harder when we offered them our autographs.

By the age of 21, I was a certified diesel mechanic and had met my future wife. Happily, Lynne shared my love of motorcycles, which was just as well, as my idea of a night out was to roar around the speedway circuit astride a Vincent sidecar, then have my date push-start my old Fordson van so I could take her home. Whether it was the sight of me in tight leathers, or the smell of racing fuel, that had Lynne smitten, I don't know, but six weeks after our first date we married.

Eventually I outgrew racing, being attracted more towards vintage motorcycles. Over the years, I painstakingly restored a 1924 single and a 1922 800cc V-twin AJS, adding a sidecar to the larger bike for family holidays and regional rallies, and a 1970 Kawasaki H1 Triple, the fastest motorcycle of its time.

Ron on his N-Zeta

I also rebuilt a 1950 Norman motorcycle for Lynne. On the first outing her bell-bottom trousers tangled in the chain, bringing the bike to an abrupt stop at the traffic lights. Mortified, she tried to drag the bike — still attached to her leg — away from eyeshot of bemused motorists. With the assistance of a bystander who had raced inside for a breadknife, she extricated herself from the chain and rode home with one trouser leg hacked off at the knee. It was some time before I could persuade her to ride on her own again.

A customer of the garage where I worked stopped by one day and was quite taken when he saw me tinkering with my AJS and sidecar.

'I have the remains of an old four-cylinder motorcycle I rescued from a disused sawmill,' he said. 'I don't know what it is, but, from the looks of your splendid restoration of this one, I reckon you could do something with it. Would you be interested in coming around and taking a look?'

Four-cylinder machines were rare and my interest was piqued. Most of the bike was missing, but I accepted the challenge and promised to let my benefactor know when I had identified the bike.

Only after I'd loaded the rusty engine and cradle into the car did I consider Lynne's reaction to another pile of junk being added to my growing collection. With all the sensitivity of a new-age man, I stopped off on the way home to buy a box of her favourite chocolates.

The Dream

Initially, the marque of the bike had me stumped. I'd never seen a configuration like it. Only the letters FN stamped on the magneto offered a clue. I leafed through old motorcycle magazines to find that the engine and frame I had acquired belonged to a Belgian 4-cylinder, inlet-over exhaust, shaft-drive Fabrique Nationale (FN). I pinpointed the year of manufacture to 1910. FN Belgium was established in 1899 to make arms and ammunition, and from 1901 to 1967 the company also produced motorcycles. Beginning in 1905 it was the first manufacturer of in-line, 4-cylinder machines.

I told the previous owner of my findings, boasting, 'I'm riding the bike back to Belgium for its centenary'. He looked dubious. I was then 26 years old. Had I known that I would be 68 before I'd attempt such a feat, I might not have been so cocky.

An article I found in the archives of New Zealand's *Ashburton Guardian* newspaper, told me the 1910 model had taken the world by storm, and that 400 FNs had been ordered by the New Zealand agency. As far as I could gather, only one other, also unrestored, was still in the country.

The frame and engine languished in the garage for many years. Only when we moved to Australia did I write to the FN factory asking for information. I was thrilled to receive a parts manual, in French, and photos, taken at the 1910 Paris Motor show, of lefthand and righthand views of that year's model.

With a renewed sense of purpose, I spent evenings working on a 1940s flat-belt Colchester lathe making replacements for damaged or missing parts. I scaled them from the photographs. The parts included the hand controls, fuel gauge, fuel and oil caps, fuel filter, oil pump and dripper.

The pedal chain was made using old racing pushbike chains of the same style but of narrower design. I machined the rear brake drum from a solid block of steel. Kevin, a skilled machinist in Tasmania, replicated the crown wheel from the badly broken sample. The bike frame was repaired using Reynolds tubing.

Leon, a fellow enthusiast from South Australia, supplied the front forks, and I made all-new sliding links to suit. Rims were bought as blanks and a tool was made to dimple and drill them. I used a cardboard template for the pattern of the oil tank and then formed it from a sheet of brass.

Leather tool bags and the seat were crafted by hand. I reconditioned engine parts and replaced the original cast-iron pistons with aluminium because modern rings would prove more efficient and easier to obtain.

The process of accurately replicating the parts was painfully slow, and several years passed before the bike started to look like one.

Meanwhile, two Honda motorcycles — a beautiful 1976 LTD GoldWing and a brand-new CX500 — were added to our stable of machines. Lynne, having erased the Norman from her memory, now wanted a bike of her own. The bright red V-twin fitted the bill perfectly.

Our son Mark raced motocross bikes, and at times I joined him on the track. I never gained a podium finish, but I did share in the exhilaration of clearing the jumps. No matter what style of riding I try, I love them all.

When our youngsters left home, Lynne and I set off on a new adventure. We rode from Alaska to Brazil on the GoldWing, a camper trailer in tow. In three years, we covered 200,000 kilometres and passed through 21 countries. That journey instilled in us a love of travel, and it taught us a great deal about the grit required to commit to such ventures. It also strengthened my resolve to ride the FN back to Belgium.

Over the years, as I studied the bike's history I became fascinated with such a marvel of engineering. In 1905, when other manufacturers were using twisted rawhide drive belts, FN began fitting a far superior beveled drive to the rear wheel. Unlike other machines, which constantly needed adjustment to stop the belt slipping, the 362cc 4-cylinder shaft-drive required no daily maintenance and was not adversely affected by wet weather. The FN was also smoother running than single and twin-cylinder machines, and its uniquely designed front suspension proved highly effective.

These pioneer machines had magneto ignition and a five-bearing crankshaft with pedal assist. LPA (light pedal assist) was required for inclines as there was no gearbox fitted as standard equipment. The lubrication was total loss, in-as-much as the oil was not returned to the oil tank, and was drained periodically from the engine. For inclines, a hand oil pump supplemented the adjustable drip-feed system. Many bikes around this period had only one or the other. And, I believe it was the only motorcycle of the time to be fitted with a fuel gauge.

Interestingly, in 1909, Percy Pierce, son of the Pierce-Arrow Motor Car Company's founder, began manufacturing 4-cylinder motorcycles very similar in design to the FN he had purchased and ridden in Europe. The earliest of the Pierce motorcycles offered a larger 688cc engine, though few were ever produced.

I wrote to other FN enthusiasts across Europe and began seriously looking at how I could realise my dream. Thanks to Jacques, Belgium's FN guru, I had photos and information to accurately complete my restoration. By this time, 2007, our children, Nikki and Mark, were married with families of their own, Lynne and I were living in Bali — the FN's centenary was fast approaching.

The FN's motor was running, but a good deal of fine-tuning was still needed. Each time I road-tested the bike, I took my life in my hands. Unsafe roads and the devil-may-care attitude of Indonesian bike riders made riding a veteran machine a nightmare. But my outings proved invaluable. I became adept at missing chickens, cows and potholes; and I learnt to avoid motorcyclists who made illegal turns across four lanes of traffic, and others talking on mobiles while holding ladders, panes of glass, even babies.

It soon became obvious that a clutch would make life much easier, given that the FN had a fixed gear and a long-wheel base. Handling, especially on corners, was proving diabolical with a bike whose slowest speed was 30kmh. The cost of a clutch from Europe was prohibitive, so it was a swap of unwanted FN parts with an online trader that allowed me to meet this challenge.

After months of anxious waiting, the clutch arrived. It took several attempts before I had it working efficiently. Each attempt meant having to remove the engine and experiment with various seals to eliminate leaks. Finally I was satisfied. And, with a little ingenuity, I fashioned tiny oilcans featuring the FN emblem, to be used to lubricate the valves and fork pivots. Similar in shape to those used on old sewing machines, the oilcans were devised by making a die, the necessary curvature being achieved by molding the bottoms of aerosol cans.

Bali to Belgium had a nice ring to it. I applied for a permit to register the bike so I could begin my journey from Indonesia. The police refused to issue a licence on the grounds that the bike was too old. For a fee, many locals offered to help, saying they knew someone in government or the military, or insisted they had connections to the local bikie club's tea lady, who could guarantee success. This was Bali, where truth never gets in the way of making a fast buck.

Even taking the bike out on the road meant risking confiscation. Registered or not, motorcycles, it was well known, were often impounded until 'duty' had been collected. I flew to Jakarta to plead my case with the police chief and came back with a letter of support from his department. But it was no help; the FN still didn't get registered. It seemed that I either lacked the right credentials or wasn't seen to be playing the game.

As a result of all the stuffing about, I missed out on celebrating the bike's centenary in Belgium. I was ticked off. Then I heard of the Fabrique Nationale Treffen that is held annually in Germany, and that 2012 was its tenth anniversary. Come hell or high water, I was determined to get to that celebration. With an overland route from Indonesia now out of the question, I had to consider my options.

The immediate solution was to return to Australia. After five years of living in Asia, Lynne and I had found it way too challenging. We had built a retirement villa in a seemingly idyllic location, complete with swimming pool and tropical gardens. But we never felt at home as expats in Bali. I was approaching 70 and fast running out of time to achieve my goal, so putting our house on the market and leaving the island was a no-brainer.

The plan was that I would return to Brisbane and Lynne would follow when the house sold. In a volatile real estate market, I knew that might take time. Never-the-less, Lynne urged me to leave, confident she'd be okay and that the right buyer would soon come along.

Before I could take the FN back, I needed permission from Australian Customs. Fortunately, I had retained the export documents that proved it was exempt from duty, so approval was quickly granted. All that was left to do was to organise the crating of the FN and take it to the air-cargo handlers. It was when the FN went through their x-ray machine that things became challenging.

A phone call from the cargo depot told me four suspect 'canisters' had been detected in the consignment. 'Don't open the crate or touch anything until I get there,' I pleaded. I'd screwed the crate together and deliberately painted the screws so that I could tell if the container had been tampered with. 'No, we won't, Mr Ron,' the agent promised.

I battled my way to the airport through heavy traffic and arrived to find the crate broken open — precisely what I didn't want to happen. All the x-ray had revealed were the FN's four engine cylinders!

I secured the crate and returned home, insisting as I left that they call me if there were further concerns. An hour later the phone rang: 'The spark plugs are dangerous and need to be removed in case they catch fire.' I tried to reason with him. Getting nowhere, I again pleaded for an assurance that they would not touch anything until I arrived back at the airport.

When I walked into the freight depot, the crate lay open and, to my horror, even the tyres had been deflated, which meant there was a good chance they would come off the rims. That could mean the bead would be dislodged, making it awkward to refit the tyres.

'The air in the tyres is not safe, Mr Ron...' I cut him off, snapping, 'The bloody bike was flown to Bali by the same airline with the tyres inflated. Nothing has changed'.

His inane smile in response had me shaking with anger. Apart from the absurdity of the claim, I was concerned at the prospect of drugs being stowed in the crate. Until the plane touched down in Brisbane, and Customs had carried out a thorough search, I knew I wouldn't rest easy.

3

The Paper Trail

I needn't have worried, the FN arrived back in Australia without further incident. I followed, and Lynne joined me shortly after. Preparations for my journey could begin in earnest. For the first time in years, I basked in the joy of sealed roads, smooth-flowing traffic, no rabid dogs, and no obvious graft.

The next 12 months were spent house-sitting, while Lynne planned my journey and I joined in local club runs to get to know my machine better. Its performance seemed to change day by day, much like my riding ability. Getting to grips with its idiosyncrasies — such as tackling hills without gears and stopping without efficient brakes at intersections — proved perplexing. On one ride, in full view of a policeman pointing a radar camera, I slid to a halt at a compulsory stop, both feet scraping on the ground.

Well at least I wasn't speeding, I thought with relief. When the officer sauntered over, I assumed he wanted to check out my old bike. I was gobsmacked when he proceeded to write an infringement notice! 'But, the bike's 100 years old, and it's impossible to stop it on a dime,' I protested. The front wheel was barely inches across the line. 'That's your problem,' he replied, not batting an eyelid. A fine of several hundred dollars woke me to the fact I'd been out of Australia way too long.

I tested the FN in winter on the icy roads of Tasmania, riding 12 kilometres to the summit of Mt. Wellington. The bike handled the conditions well, but after pushing it for one kilometre, I could see I needed to get myself in shape if I was going to survive the ride across a third of the world's circumference.

With a bit of practice, I found I could push-start the bike in less than a metre. This meant no more pedaling, or spinning the back wheel to start, which was hard work, especially under a heavy load.

Another thing to learn was to change the back tyre more efficiently. Because the beaded-edge back tyre had blown a couple of times and jumped off the rim and jammed up inside the mudguard, I played around with air pressures. It may have been that the tyre hadn't been correctly fitted, or that the tube was under-inflated. Some brands notoriously have weak sidewalls. I could only guess at what was the safest air pressure.

I'd been following the adventures of Britain's Tim Scott. Riding a 1920s FN in the 2010 Peking-to-Paris, he was plagued with broken spokes and differential problems. Would I get the same problems, especially as my machine was more than 10 years older?

With so little carrying capacity, it was tough deciding on my final list of essentials. Extra spokes were imperative, and a couple of spare carburettor jets were necessary to correct fuel problems. I made an all-purpose, multi-fit spanner to limit the size of the tool kit. At 200 grams, it was the weight required to test the inlet-valve springs. These need to open one millimetre when this weight is applied to the end of the valve stem. Just to be on the safe side, I had the magneto rewound after it flooded during a heavy downpour.

The new valve springs I had made proved to be too darned strong to open, thus preventing the engine from starting. At the eleventh hour, I got the manufacturer to make another 50. Thankfully, this time they worked perfectly. So far, I'd clocked up 2,000 kilometres. If such a thing were possible, the engine was, by now, fine-tuned. I felt I had done all I could to make my little bike roadworthy.

I had decided I'd start from Nepal as it was known to be easier to clear a vehicle through customs than India. Lynne pored over maps, measured distances, made notes, and read up on other travel odysseys. These were mostly accounts by young men on KTMs, Teneres and Africa Twins, all bikes far better suited to rough terrain than my FN. Their big advantages were huge petrol tanks, GPS, laptops, enormous saddlebags and wide tyres.

Lynne and I had always travelled with the kitchen sink, but this time I wanted to rely solely on my wits and carry as little as possible. And space was at a premium. The dilemma was not so much what to take but where to stow it.

Mindful of keeping everything to a minimum for my 100-kilogram machine, and for ease of removal, we carefully sourced clothing, camping gear and panniers. Somehow, the list kept growing. All I could bring myself to throw out were cable ties and a roll of gasket paper. I really was playing with myself thinking the 20 grams these items weighed was going to make a difference.

The bags I would carry needed to be waterproof and lightweight, yet strong enough to withstand constant use. The soft panniers I had made in Bali soon fell apart under pressure, so I replaced them with a more robust, yet soft, Dry Rider set. Although I'd have been happy wearing Crocs, I had to admit they wouldn't offer much protection and settled instead, on a sturdy pair of waterproof boots.

Enormous advances have been made in electronics since the 1980s, when Lynne and I travelled from the top of the world to the bottom. We'd spent three years riding from Alaska to Brazil, covering every state of America, Canada, Mexico, Central and South America. For this trip, I decided I had to limit myself to a camera, a mobile phone and a solar-charger, a gift from Mark. Only 100 millimetres long, it could fully charge my iPhone in an hour in a power socket, and in less than four hours in the sun. Other gadgets were tempting, but I just didn't have room.

When our daughter, Nikki, created a blog — www.oldblokeonabike. com — we were posting entries and attracting interest from across the globe even before I left. I chose not to seek major sponsorship, realising that my focus would have to be on the job at hand, not spruiking the qualities of various products. I did, however, appreciate a smart polo shirt and a discounted fare from Thai Airways to ship the bike and me to Nepal, in return for endorsing their product.

The Carnet de Passage (temporary import document), for the bike was secured through the Royal Automobile Association. When Lynne and I travelled abroad in 1986 on our GoldWing, we had to mortgage our home as a guarantee that we would return the bike to Australia. This time, I only needed to pay a $1000 bond, part of which would be refunded when it returned home. Not all countries require a carnet, but India and Iran demand bonds of 400-500 percent of a bike's value. This fee removes any incentive for travellers to sell their machines along the way should they find themselves short of cash or decide to bring their travels to a halt.

I delivered the FN, and the lightweight steel crate I had made to ship it in, to the Thai Airways' cargo agent a week before departure. Airfreight was calculated either on volume or weight, whichever cost was greater.

The motorcycle needed degassing before it could be shipped because it was classified as dangerous goods. To save a few dollars, I ran a hose from my car's exhaust pipe into the fuel tank of the bike and left the car idling for 20 minutes, thus rendering the tank non-flammable.

Australian Customs stamped the carnet and gave the green light. I put the bike, all my gear and three spare tyres in the crate, quietly confident they would be there on my arrival in Kathmandu. This time, there was no stuffing about, everything going as smooth as clockwork.

Vehicle insurance was something I'd never considered previously, but it was now mandatory in most of the countries I would visit. Insurance wouldn't have meant much if I had an accident. The truth is, compulsory insurance is just another form of revenue collecting.

Medical insurance, though, is a different kettle of fish. I consider this to be essential — and it doesn't come cheap. But chances of being in a collision were very real. I thought about a friend who had gone on a motorcycle tour in India and had been hit from behind. She barely escaped with her life.

I'd had my share of tempting Lady Luck over the years: speedway riding and road racing had been risky; and lighting a fire under a friend's house to rid it of rats had been a tad suicidal. So, figuring that I was ahead on points, the insurance cost to be flown home and put back together, should the need arise, was a small price to pay. I saw it as no big deal. It was falling into the Ganges that really scared the bejesus out of me!

So far the trip had cost $6,000. Figuring on spending $50 a day, I intended to camp out often and eat at places frequented by locals.

In the final few days before departure, I was as restless as a drummer with a boil on his bum. Bags were packed and unpacked, and my itinerary was checked and rechecked. Visas had been applied for well in advance, the timing for each being critical. So much depended on how many miles I could do in a day, and whether a visa could be extended. Excitement cranked up a notch when the visa for India arrived.

I waited anxiously for my Pakistani visa. In desperation, I phoned the embassy in Canberra because Pakistan consular staff had my passport, and without it, I wouldn't be going anywhere. 'I'm sorry, sir, we cannot send it until you tell us where you'll be staying in Pakistan,' the official said politely. I directed him to my blog site, explaining that I didn't have a clue where I might be sleeping, and promised I had no intention of overstaying. I was on a mission, I said, and I didn't plan on being in any country longer than necessary. My passport, complete with an impressive visa was hand-delivered next day.

The visa for Iran, I was told, once it had been approved, would be waiting for me in Lahore. This was because, with Western embargoes on Iran, it couldn't be issued in Australia, and money could not be paid to the

Canberra embassy. With a little ingenuity, we circumvented this obstacle via an agent in Britain and a bank in Turkey. A magical number would be sent from Iran's foreign affairs department, and this would be forwarded to the nominated consular office. I wasn't about to let politics get in the way of my plans. I kept my fingers crossed that Australia wouldn't stuff things up by imposing further sanctions on Iran. The visa for Nepal would be procured on entry, that being a cheaper option than applying for it outside the country.

Friends and family organised a lunch in Brisbane. It was a moving send-off. Like all goodbyes, this one was bittersweet, but I felt optimistic I'd return safe and sound. That night, I repacked my luggage one last time — just in case.

On Sunday, February 5, 2012, I left Brisbane. Lynne was to meet me in India in a few weeks. While I made my way south from Nepal, crossed the border and headed to Uttar Pradesh, she would fly to Delhi and travel by train to Agra, where we would spend a few days together. Lynne was keen to explore Rajasthan, and as my route would take me west through the state, this would provide a good opportunity for us to meet from time to time, and combine a little sightseeing with the day-to-day tasks that were bound to catch up with me.

So there were no teary farewells, just a long wait at the airport and a quick look back and a wave before boarding the flight to Thailand.

Nine hours later I arrived in steamy Bangkok. 'Welcome, Mr Ron, my name is Noodle,' beamed the manager of the Airport Hotel. I found his moniker as amusing as the Thai characters on my room's computer keyboard. There was no way I would be able to send emails. Thankfully, I didn't need to. Lynne called with last-minute instructions: be careful of pickpockets, avoid rabid dogs, and only eat cooked food. I promised to follow her advice.

Next morning, after a hearty bowl of thick rice porridge, I headed to the new Suvarnabhumi Airport for my connecting flight to Nepal. In just over three hours we descended into the narrow Kathmandu Valley with brief glimpses of the majestic Himalayas rising through the clouds. A gentle bump, the reverse-thrust scream, and the plane rolled to a halt. I'd arrived at the top of the world.

When the chap seated next to me asked why I had chosen to start my journey in Nepal, I replied, brightly, 'Because, I will be riding all downhill from here!'

Bike arrives safely in its crate - Nepal

Downhill from here - Nepal

17

4

On Top of the World

The cold air packed a punch, and the heavy grey blanket hanging low over the world's third-most polluted city threatened to swallow me whole. It might have been kinder to my lungs to stay on the plane.

Before going to find the FN, I searched for a phone-card seller.

'I need to have your photo for our records,' he said, yet barely glanced at my faded passport shot. It fazed him not at all that I was now grey-haired and a score years older. A photo of the flying nun would have satisfied him.

The clerk at Thai Airlines did the paperwork on a 'Hemingway' typewriter — an ideal contraption considering Nepal's sporadic power supply. No money changed hands, either for the bill of lading or the carnet. Soon I was cheerfully on my way. All so easy!

Even though the customs shed was only a short walk away, a pushy tout insisted that for $20 we could drive there in his friend's taxi. I refused. He stuck to me until we reached the shed, where he made one last attempt to get paid just for accompanying me. I sensed challenging times ahead.

Despite repeated checks at the counter, for two hours customs officials shuffled paperwork. Two men took me aside, and, out of earshot of the counter staff, told me what it would cost to get my bike released. I guessed they were brokers, and that the real amount was much less.

It reminded me of how often this scenario is played out the world over. The game is to keep the sucker waiting for as long as possible. Then, when his resistance is low and he's running out of time, hit him with a charge they think he'll accept. Call it baksheesh, a bribe, an honest-to-god fee, whatever — it all adds up to the same. In Nepal, Cancun or Timbuktu, wherever, it's money that makes the wheels go round. Nothing is ever free, no matter which god one prays to.

I glanced nervously at the time, then said I would leave the bike and collect it next morning.

'No, no. Paperwork is cleared. Cannot store. You must take now.'

I argued that there wasn't time to assemble the bike before the warehouse closed at five o'clock. He shrugged, went into his office, and closed the door.

The FN's handlebars, controls and pedal gear had been removed in Brisbane to keep the crate as small as possible. Reassembling it, with every man and his yak getting in the way, wasn't easy. Each took a turn at passing me tools I didn't need; and each just had to check that the horn worked. My patience was being sorely tested. No sooner had I unbolted the metal crate than it vanished. The Nepalese know a bargain when they see one. No doubt the container would be sold for a tidy sum.

Caught up in the urgency of the moment and suffering the effects of high altitude, I was all fingers and thumbs. The gas tank had been emptied before the flight, so I needed fuel. All the fuel outlets in the city seemed to be waiting for a delivery. *What now!* One fellow finally relented and parted with two litres from his own bike — at an exorbitant price. But at least I could get on my way.

The FN started first time. After a short warm up, I was hustled out the door, still cramming luggage aboard as I went. I'd been told to show my paperwork at the exit checkpoint, but I wasn't stopping. I played dumb, gave the security guard a wave, and rode on.

It quickly became apparent that I had brought far too much gear, but at this stage, I had no idea what to dump — or even which way to travel. I turned my pockets inside out trying to find where I'd written the address for the first night's accommodation. The hotel was in Thamel somewhere. The signs, of course, were all in Nepalese. As luck would have it, there were two Thamels — and I was not going to make it to either before nightfall.

The bike stalled repeatedly because of water in the fuel. With traffic jostling around me, and horns blaring, I struggled to push the bike onto the footpath to drain the carburettor before I could re-enter the fray. At low speed, and with under-inflated tyres, the FN handled poorly under its excess load. And I wasn't faring much better.

As twilight deepened, the risk of being on the road increased. I had once ridden after dark in Bolivia and almost run into a rope strung across the road. I swore I'd never be that dumb again. I stopped to weigh my options, my knees trembling. The mix of thin air and heady excitement were catching up with me.

'Can I be of assistance, mister?' a stranger asked.

I explained my problem.

'It's not safe to stop here after dark,' he warned. 'Better you come to my guesthouse. It's not far.'

My head bobbed like a dashboard dog. I was grateful for the offer and too weary to argue. Together, we pushed the FN two kilometres before heaving it into the hotel foyer and pushing it out of sight.

The room was small, the shower cold and the bed hard, but at least everything was clean. I barely managed to charge my mobile phone before the hum of generators signalled the power had gone off. Exhausted, I switched off the light, lay on the narrow cot and closed my eyes. I'd just drifted off when there was a knock on the door.

'Here, Mr Ron, something for you to eat,' said the manager, grinning broadly. I thanked him for the packet of orange biscuits and crawled back into bed, appreciative of the gesture but desperate for sleep.

First of the climbs - Nepal

Immediately after breakfast, armed with two jerry cans, I went in search of petrol. I met an English-speaking taxi driver at a street corner, and for the next two hours we drove all over town, squeezing through narrow alleyways and knocking on door after door.

I'd ask, 'Do you have any benzine for sale?' and always, from chubby faces peering out beneath richly-patterned tasselled hats, came the reply, 'Chaina' (No). Householders in Nepal, I learned, squirrel away whatever petrol they can get their hands on, either for their own use or to sell on the black market. Today, no one was sharing.

Across the city, tangled webs of power lines link the buildings. Each morning, amid a constant cacophony, street cleaners sweep away yesterday's odorous residue, while fruit vendors busily trade from their bicycles.

At every intersection, two-stroke bikes jockey for position. In an effort to reduce the smog the prime minister, Baburam Bhattarai, had ordered military personnel to use bicycles as transport at least one day a week. So pervasive was the pollution, it was hard to tell if his decree was making any difference.

'Stay here,' my friendly taxi driver ordered. 'When they see you they don't sell.' Soon he came back from around a corner with six litres. In a way, he was probably right — except that we were now at a gas station! Although I paid twice the going rate, I was relieved I could at last get on my way. The delays were driving me nuts.

Back at the hotel, the bill for the night had my eyebrows raised. 'I'm giving it to you cheaper because you're old,' declared the manager, pointing to the ledger's list of names and prices paid. I thanked him and shook his hand. With hindsight, I should have checked the tariff first. Ah well, another lesson learned.

Before leaving Kathmandu, I needed to clarify the way to Pokhara. It was impossible to read maps on the iPhone, so I resorted to asking locals for directions. I figured I'd be right when two people pointed the same way.

Even with the luggage strapped on firmly, riding was difficult. Pedestrians and motorcycles darted in and out. I'd move a metre or two, then stop, move again, then stop . . . This didn't sit well with the FN, and I hadn't yet twigged the benefit of saving the clutch by turning off the engine and push-starting. I was about to learn the hard way.

Amid the mayhem — and with my nerves strung out — I felt the clutch slip. I pulled over to adjust it. That was when I discovered that the substitute fibre plates I was using were not up to the job. Wiping the sweat from my brow, I asked people gathering around if I could take the bike apart on the footpath. Everyone agreed, 'Yes, yes, no problem.'

Of course, it was a problem for the owner of the shop in front of which I was doing my repairs. When he turned up, he basically told me to remove all the crap off his step and bugger off!

The parts were snatched up and spread on newspaper on the dusty road, no longer in any semblence of order. Thankfully, Yogendra and Hari, two local mechanics who had helped me remove the motor, took the clutch plates away. They ground them on a piece of concrete until the steel was clear of fibre. The FN normally uses 15 steel clutch plates, and I had replaced six of these with fibre plates to create a softer clutch. Fortunately, I carried the original steel plates with me as spares, so all was not lost. But I did break an engine mount in the process.

I was back on the road within three hours. The two young men who had helped refused payment and waved me on my way. For the rest of the day, I rode on extremely steep, potholed roads. One seriously precipitous section took half an hour to negotiate. I shuddered at the thought of riding in the opposite direction.

By now, the traffic was thinning. I passed two buses embracing each other after a head-on collision. I would soon become used to sights like this. Gripping the handlebars even more tightly, and trying to balance a spare fuel-can on the tank, I focused on keeping the bike upright.

As I rounded a bend on one sharp descent, the fuel can tottered and slid on to the road. By the time I had propped the bike against a post and scurried back, a car had run over the funnel of the plastic container, thus rendering it useless. *Bugger!*

Seventy-three kilometres from Kathmandu, I began searching for a place to spend the night. With great relief, I came across the Pokhara Guesthouse. Crowds of onlookers quickly gathered, eager to pose beside the FN and have their pictures taken with mobile phones. The name of the guesthouse proved a misnomer: I still had to travel nearly twice as far to get to Pokhara.

The English-speaking hosts were welcoming, and I was served a satisfying meal of chicken stew, rice and potatoes. It was just what I needed after such an exhausting day.

Ohading, a local schoolteacher, brought his class along to inspect the bike. Most of the children spoke English, and they were curious.

'Where are you from?'

'How old are you?'

'Where are you going?'

'How old is the bike?'

'Where is your wife?'

I wondered how many times in the months ahead I'd be subjected to such interrogations.

When Lynne Skyped me that evening, and heard of the day's hassles, she suggested I chalk it up as my initiation. She said that having survived the trials of the previous two days the rest of the journey would be a breeze. She knew I just needed to vent.

I told her the highway congestion was much like Bali's, but then admitted that a conversation I'd had with a chap who'd ridden across the subcontinent had put the wind up me a little. 'Nepal is a piece of cake,' he'd boasted. 'Wait until you reach India. It's fucking insane.'

I decided, that if that were true, then I'd better stop complaining and enjoy the easy going while it lasted! Better to focus on tackling one day at a time — and remember to breathe deeply. There's a level of comfort in going to bed believing tomorrow will be a better day, but things rarely turn out the way we expect.

Dark clouds gathered overnight, and when I set out for Pokhara early next morning, the storm hit with a vengeance. The FN started well initially, but when the motor became saturated it died. I tried rolling it downhill, but it refused to start again until I took shelter and dried the spark plugs and distributor. I don't mind riding in rain, but this was over the top, especially with the electrics constantly dying on me.

My Huskie gear stood up to the elements for nearly four hours, which was remarkable considering the deluge. Eventually though, moisture began to seep through the seams, and my fancy waterproof boots also gave up the ghost. I refused to give in. Hunched down low over the tank, I was barely able to see a thing through the pissing rain.

The road had broken up so badly on one stretch that I could only travel at 15 kmh. I counted the wreckage of about a score of vehicles along the way. At 3.00 pm, after eight hours of torture, I crawled into Pokhara, chilled and bone weary.

Ten minutes under a scalding hot shower had me rejuvenated. From the hotel roof, I took in the view. For the first time, I began to appreciate my surroundings. The weather had cleared, revealing neatly cultivated valleys backed by majestic snow-capped ranges. It began to sink in: I was in the Himalayas, at the top of the world. Elated, I knew that life doesn't get much more spectacular than this.

Mountain views - Nepal

Tight passing - Nepal

5

The Long Way Down

Fuel continued to be a problem. I spent hours trudging around Pokhara in a vain search, until an almond-eyed girl offered to help. Together, Pumam and I visited several outlets on her scooter. Eventually, one invited us to come back at 6.00 pm, when a delivery was due. We returned, and got to fill the tank plus 10 more litres.

The winding, mountainous road to the Indian border town of Palpa was in good condition — well, it was good for this part of the world. Even with light traffic, it still took me nine hours to travel 160 kilometres. Over the worst sections, I pedalled and pushed up more than 20 hills. My head pounded in the thin mountain air, and my legs trembled with relief as we reached each summit. The FN valiantly took them all, bar one, in her stride. On that occasion, I paid a passerby to help push the final 20 metres. It was money well spent.

With some of the world's highest mountains as a backdrop, and a steely grey river snaking far below, I couldn't help but be impressed by the stunning beauty around me. Pastel-coloured houses and neatly tended vegetable plots dotted the hillsides. As tempting as it was to take lots of photos, it was difficult to stop because there was rarely anywhere to park safely.

Once, when negotiating my way through a convoy of trucks, one driver decided to reverse, missing the bike by centimetres. My shouts fell on deaf ears. Only when his passenger jumped down from the cab to give directions was I noticed jammed between the truck and cliff face. His incredulous stare attested to my narrow escape. I leant against the bank and waited for my heart to stop pounding before I pushed off again.

At Palpa, Nepalese customs stamped my passport, then insisted I get a copy made for them. I followed their directions to a printer. An hour-

and-a-half later, when the power came back on, I got the copy. I had chosen this route to avoid the endless paperwork and long delays usually encountered at busier border crossings. Something wasn't working.

On the Butwal side of the border, it was election time and the immigration office was closed until 1.00 pm. A strong military presence persuaded me that taking photographs wouldn't be welcome. While I sat and waited, the tea wallah was sent to get refreshments. When he returned, with hot tea and ginger-nut biscuits, I was contemplating a vast compound full of derelict trucks, motorcycles, and 4WDs.

'Why are all these vehicles here?' I asked. 'Where did they come from?'

'Many travellers with no papers,' he replied, his head wagging rhythmically side to side, 'so police lock up their transport.'

Each vehicle, tyres flat, bodywork weathered and dusty, stood testament to unfilled overland dreams.

Finally, with the immigration officers back on the job, my carnet was stamped. Soon after being cleared through customs and getting back on the road, I ran into trouble. The valve springs started to collapse, each incident marked by a change in engine noise before power fell away and the bike stopped. After a few collapses, it took me only 15 minutes to remove the manifold, locate the offending spring (sometimes it had been sucked into the engine), either stretch or replace it, and fit a new clip to secure the spring.

The springs were not my only problem. Suddenly there was an almighty bang: it was the back tyre flying off the rim. I was careering about the road and, in panic, I tried using the back-pedal brake. *Damn, it didn't work!*

Even the steel rim skating along the ground, sparks flying, did little to slow me. My heart was in my mouth as I clung on, afraid of being hit by oncoming vehicles. Finally we ground to a halt. I staggered off, dizzy and shaking.

In the stifling heat, replacing the tyre was a struggle, worsened by passersby crowding in for a better look. Everyone offered advice, in a mixture of English and Hindi, on how I should do the job. Before I could get the wheel out, the bike had to be jacked up with a rock under the engine so that the stand could be removed. For once, having helpers there to steady the machine was a blessing.

When the repairs were complete, I pointed to a name on a scrap of paper and asked, wearily, 'Where will I find this hotel?'

'That way,' volunteered a man with a fierce moustache. Several others nodded, but it was clear not everyone was in agreement.

'So what do you suggest?' I asked. An elderly gent in a pristine white kurta tugged at my sleeve: 'Sir, sir, let me show you a very, very good hotel.'

A discussion ensued and I looked on expectantly, wishing I hadn't opened my big mouth. A sea of arms, like an animated Lord Vishnu, pointed in every direction. Why was everything proving to be so damn hard?

'It must be clean,' I insisted. 'I need a clean hotel with plenty of hot water.' Judging by the looks I received, I might as well have been asking if it was safe to swim in the Ganges.

The hostelries Lynne and I had sourced before leaving home were often impossible to locate. Such places were rarely advertised and locals weren't familiar with hotels geared to the tourist industry. Originally, I'd hoped to save money by camping, but I was kidding myself if I thought I could erect a tent. In fact, it was ridiculous to imagine camping anywhere in India outside of national parks. I smiled at my ignorance.

One downside of using hotels was Indians' penchant for ledger-keeping. I'd love a dollar for every time I had to sign my name. In one lodging, my signature went on the register 18 times.

The hotel voted the best by the head-bobbing crowd was ghastly, but it was too late in the day to search for another. I took one look at the room and recoiled in disgust. To hide a patchwork of filthy stains, I threw the bike cover over the bed and spread out my sleeping bag. Despite the grim conditions, there was a shower, but only after I'd cleared a bird's nest of hair and other unmentionables from the drain.

The day's grime flushed away, it was great to be clean and to put on fresh but crumpled clothes. As I poked another hole in my belt, I had to accept that all the pedalling, to which I was unaccustomed, was taking its toll. At this rate, I'd be pipe-cleaner thin by the time I got to Belgium.

My route was to take me, via Basti, to Barabanki. I left at 5.00 am, and in the poor light I failed to notice there were two towns with the same name. You guessed: I chose the wrong one.

Sixty kilometres off course, and with me pushing hard to make up for lost time, the bike suffered a seizure on the number-one cylinder. I dismantled the engine on the side of the road, the usual horde of onlookers appearing from nowhere to stare in amazement as I laid out the parts in some semblance of order.

'Can someone find me a hammer?' I appealed to the crowd. One chap returned with a hefty mallet, which, despite its size, worked better than the rock I'd been using to drive out the gudgeon pin. I managed to file off the fused pieces of aluminium and was relieved to find no other visible damage. All the while, the onlookers chatted among themselves, picking up parts, examining and passing them back and forth. So great was the interest, I might have been a visitor from Mars.

Eventually, the bike was back together, and a quick shove helped me on my way. Two days into India and already I had broken down several times. Hoping this wasn't an omen for the rest of the journey, I remained optimistic that keeping the FN going was achievable. My years of playing around with engines had taught me plenty. Without those mechanical skills, life would have been a whole lot tougher.

Almost from the moment I crossed the border, I recognised how much that religion is integral to life in India: ceremony takes precedence over everything. I found myself caught in processions even when I had no intention of joining in. One minute I'd be on my own — if such a thing is possible in India — the next I'd be surrounded by chanting devotees carrying banners and brilliantly decorated effigies. Everyone ambled along, in lengthy processions, oblivious to the traffic, which could be held up for hours.

The FN, too, was sometimes a traffic stopper. Motorists would drive alongside to gape at the bike and take pictures on their phones. The curiosity was to be expected, but when drivers swerved in front of the bike without warning it reminded me of the constant peril I faced. Someone once tried to tell me that life in India is not accorded much value. It is hard to imagine that drivers have a death wish, but, as in Bali, they certainly don't appear to have any idea how dangerous their manoeuvres are. Already I was acutely aware that I was on a trip not for the faint-hearted!

6

One Born Every Minute

Each morning, the same routine: stretch inlet-valve springs; check tyre inflation; remove grit and water from carburettor bowl and jet. It was puzzling me that the contact points in the magneto were widening quickly yet reducing engine performance. This is the opposite of what normally happens.

And I had a funding problem. At first, I hadn't realised it would be impossible to change foreign currency in small towns and villages. Therefore, I had to manage my ready cash so that, when it started to run low, I had to be within reach of a city — which meant that I then had to struggle through seemingly endless traffic congestion to find a bank.

In one city, just as I had negotiated my way around a moving truck, the engine stopped. Again! This time it was a broken magneto spring. It seemed that everything on the bike was going to need replacing at least once. Luckily, I'd foreseen this possibility and had brought along two spares fashioned from a hacksaw blade.

Much later, having left Kanpur and finally making it to the NH2 (National Highway 2), I ran into a heavy traffic jam. A truck had rolled and its load of grain was strewn across the highway. A long delay ensued. The driver cleared away the mess, while all and sundry stepped in to direct traffic. Talk about having too many chiefs and not enough Indians!

A further setback occurred when I came upon another accident. This time a pedestrian was injured and people seemed to be arguing about who was responsible. I hoped I would never cause an accident — facing an irate crowd might prove a whole lot worse than being injured.

Rather than trying to find a hotel where few decent ones existed, I hit on the idea of doing what long-distance drivers do: use dhabas. These truck stops are roadside restaurants that provide a place to wash, a hot meal and a chance for a few hours' rest on charpoys (simple, free beds, fashioned from strips of rubber tyre stretched across a frame).

For less than a dollar, I could buy a meal of bright yellow dhal, raw turnips, tomatoes, freshly made rotis (cooked in a clay oven), and a mountain of rice, all washed down with a tin mug of hot sweet tea. I carried my own plate and utensils in the hope of minimising the chances of dysentery.

The downside to dhabas: blaring horns, flashing lights and the constant hubbub of vehicles arriving and departing. No chance of a peaceful kip or of privacy, with locals peering unabashedly as I undressed. Only when squatting over the long drop — like a cat having a crap in a flowerpot — was I without an audience. And I had to remember to take my own paper.

The owner of one truck stop insisted on shouting me a few glasses of Finnish vodka that he'd scored on the blackmarket. Loath to offend, I accepted. Three hours later, I staggered to my charpoy and passed out. I'm not a drinker at the best of times, and the combination of vodka and yet another hard day on the bike had left me a goner.

Next morning I woke feeling as if I'd spent the night in a blender. I tried not to move my head any more than necessary as I nibbled on one of my last muesli bars. I couldn't face the thought of a curry breakfast. I donned freshly laundered, but still-damp thermals, which hugged my scrawny frame, and, even before I hit the tarmac, I knew it was going to be a cold, prickly ride, made worse by a throbbing hangover.

Eventually, I was in Agra where Lynne was due to meet me. It seemed so much longer than the 10 days since I had last seen her, and we had a great many amusing tales to share.

Lynne recounted her harrowing experience when catching the train from Delhi. Indian Rail, offering online bookings and boasting a fast and efficient service for six billion passengers annually, got her approving nod — until she turned up at Delhi station and found it bursting at the seams.

Gingerly, she stepped over prone figures amid luggage and assorted boxes. Dodging porters stooped under the weight of over-sized trolleys, she peered around looking for something recognisable. Urgency was in the air, everyone was on a mission: food sellers, beggars, businessmen, touts… For a lone foreigner in her granny years it was a daunting moment.

She searched for her name on the passenger lists on each carriage. When a self-assured individual strode from the booking office to render

Milk delivery - India

Rajasthani

Pipe smoker - Rajasthan

assistance, she showed him her ticket.

'This is no good,' he said shaking his head. 'You need to have your ticket authorised. This happens when tourists buy online. It's a scam. They don't add your name unless your ticket is approved.'

Clearing a path towards the exit, he urged: 'This way, quickly. It will only take us a few minutes to get to the administration office to have the ticket stamped, then I can help you get on the train.'

Lynne hesitated, then followed reluctantly, wondering if perhaps there was another office at the front of the building. Concern welled up when the man began negotiating a fare with a taxi driver. 'I don't want to go anywhere,' she objected — and was ignored.

Whack. The startled taxi driver held his hand to his face, and the rogue, feigning shock at the price, appeared to be playing the role of Sir Galahad. The two were in collusion, Lynne realised, so she turned on her heel and hurried back towards the platform.

'What are you doing?' the man barked, grabbing her arm. 'You're wasting time and I'm trying to help you.'

Lynne shook him off angrily, her heart pounding as she fought through the crush, hoping the train hadn't already left. The devil was hot on her heels, anxious that his meal ticket shouldn't disappear. 'Here it is, madam, your carriage!' he shouted triumphantly, standing in the exact same spot they'd met earlier. 'And here's your name, Mrs Lin-ett-e Fellow-es.'

Just as the whistle blew, the brazen shyster grabbed her suitcase and leapt on board, shouldering his way down the aisle towards the allocated seat. Smugly, he stowed her suitcase and backpack and waited expectantly. Against her better judgement, Lynne handed him a 50-rupee note and sank into her seat, acutely aware of passengers' watching eyes.

'Well that was a novel way to get a porter to carry your bags,' I laughed when she told me of her scare.

We later learned of other travellers' experiences — possibly even with the same con artist — where they were told the tourist office had been bombed two weeks before so they needed to go in a rickshaw to buy tickets in the city centre!

As it turned out, a charming young fellow from Gujarat sat beside Lynne on the train and they spent the journey swapping tales and laughing. When the train pulled into the Agra station, Robin ensured Lynne was safely in a taxi before he made his way to his hotel for a meeting. Next day, he visited our home-stay and I was able to thank him in person for his chivalry.

We were at the Heritage Homestay, a very different experience from what I was growing accustomed to. Despite the somewhat dubious conditions at the hotels and dhabas, so far I'd always been well treated and had no complaints. My gear was never tampered with, and I could nod off after a hard day's ride, dry and warm, feeling safe among genuinely hospitable people.

Even when the bike was surrounded by a polite mob of onlookers, they only fiddled with levers and the horn. So far nothing had been stolen. My age amazed everyone and, though only a few spoke English, we seemed to share a mutual understanding. Our host, Mr Singh, so wisely, put it this way: 'Our dress code, language and culture might be different, but we all bleed the same colour.'

Later that evening, when I removed my boots, Lynne gasped and screwed up her nose: 'What the hell has happened to your feet?'

I had started my journey wearing my sturdy pair of motorcycle boots with reinforced toecaps. In normal riding conditions, these would have been perfect. But, because of the bike's extra height, I had to press my toes into the ground for extra stability when trying to stop in heavy traffic. This added pressure had caused the nails on my big toes to blacken and become inflamed.

'Why not switch to open sandals when you're not riding?' Lynne suggested. 'It could stave off infection.' This made sense, but, hating shopping, I put her advice out of my mind. My main concern was the bike.

For the most part, it was running well, and the only problems had been minor. One worry was the amount of oil that leaked out of the exhaust-valve lifters. Oil, combined with dust and grime, coated my boots, pants, the bike and gearbags, making it difficult to keep anything clean. I did my best to set off each morning with clean gear, even if it only stayed that way for a few hours. I needed to devise a way to limit the amount of oil seepage.

Meanwhile, one of the 'seven wonders of the world' was beckoning. I'd hoped to take a photo of the FN in front of the Taj Mahal, but that wasn't going to be possible. I was informed that no traffic was permitted beyond the outer gates. It was an initiative to minimise pollution damage to the monument, easy to understand in a city suffocating under a thick cloud of smog.

Lynne and I arrived early and joined the growing throng, eager to see the magnificent white marble shrine. Being in the presence of the Taj

Mahal is as spellbinding as the architect had intended. Left and right, in front and back, global travellers posed for that once-in-a lifetime picture.

While we were setting up to frame a shot through one of the many arches, a quietly spoken gentleman in western dress approached and began what was obviously a well-rehearsed spiel: 'Sir and madam, I can show you the very best places to take your photographs. I have worked as a gardener here for the past 30 years and I know exactly where you should stand. Please, let me guide you.'

Lynne and I were dubious. We were keen to capture memorable images, but also wary that this might be another con. 'My wife's a photographer,' I told him.

'Yes she is, sir, and a very fine one too, but I can make her pictures even more beautiful — and for only a few rupees. I will share my knowledge with you, because you look like kind man. Here, stand right on this spot.' He insisted. We obliged.

For the next half-hour, our professional guide and storyteller rushed us from one end of the long halls to the other, pointing out the best angles and checking to make sure we were following his instructions. Then, when our escort deemed the tour was over, he requested $30 for the service.

We gulped: 'You said only a few rupees.'

'I'm a poor man, look at my shoes,' he complained.

'But you're hired as a gardener, right?'

'Ah yes, but a more knowledgeable gardener is impossible to find.'

We'd barely settled on a fair price before our moonlighting friend left us and started wooing his next customer, a portly American with a very large camera. 'Sir, please let me show you the very best places to take your photographs. I have worked as a gardener here for 30 years…'

Dhaba - India

After a day's tough ride - India   Dhaba time - India

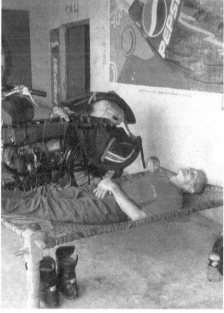

7

A Comic Opera

'Take my picture, please, mister, PLEASE.'

'You buy, you buy, very cheap, only 500 rupees.' One young voice after another called. 'My family make, very precious. Okay, for you today, my first customer, only 100 rupees.'

Although I had to admire their persistence, it seemed wise to avoid eye contact with the horde of youngsters who seemed to appear out of nowhere. Since the recent acquisition of two spare tubes, the FN was now grossly overloaded, and I couldn't take on anything else. (The tubes were not the right size, and their quality was questionable, but they could make a difference in an emergency.)

When the sightseeing was over, it was time to get down to business. Mr. Singh offered me the use of his engine-reconditioning shop to do repairs. These included inserting a small nail in the chain-adjuster clamp. This would give a better grip on the dovetail because the pedal gear frequently came loose. Rough roads had caused the brass ring on the horn bulb and light hinges to vibrate free. A strong hose clamp, though not an attractive fix, would do the job on the bulb horn; and a rubber hose over the tailpipe of the muffler would, I hoped, direct oil away from the rear tyre.

Unfortunately, when the tube had blown apart earlier, it had broken the mudguard stay, bending the guard into the carrier and taking off a large chunk of paint. Any more of this and the bike would be in need of major restoration by the end of the journey.

Lynne and I took our leave from the Singh home after a few days' rest and arranged to meet again later in Rajasthan.

Once across the state line, I was struck by several improvements. Restaurants and hotels, public toilets and signs advertising drinking water became apparent. Motorcycles were able to pass through the tollways without charge, making entries and exits easier. The four-lane highway was clean and easy to travel. At least it was until I entered each town, when rows of judder bars appeared without warning, threatening to shake the bike to pieces.

The hose extension I'd made barely lasted five kilometres before a hole appeared. The poor grade of rubber wasn't able to withstand the pressure. I needed to come up with a better design.

A few hours into the day I was jolted out of a fuddle by the driver of a timeworn Morris Oxford honking his horn and waving frantically. As the car drew alongside, a woman leant out the window and invited me to stop for a drink. Bemused, I pulled into a roadside café and the two of us made our way to a table and ordered chai. For the next hour we laughingly shared our travel experiences, much to the amusement of locals, intrigued at our strange goings-on. Before we parted, the woman suggested we rendezvous at the Hotel Atithi.

'I'm sorry, but I'm meeting my wife there,' I said kissing the lady affectionately on the cheek.

'No matter,' said Lynne, 'I'm meeting my husband, Ron. Maybe you know him?'

The little motorcycle excelled itself on the 245 kilometre-ride that day. The only problem was that the previously fractured rear-mudguard stay was now completely severed.

The instructions to get to our hotel were to look for the Radio India building and then take the next right. Inching through a belching armada of buses, trucks, taxis and motorbikes, with my eyes streaming, I searched in vain for some sign that I was on the right track. It seemed I was going in endless circles. I asked one person after another, 'Where is the Hotel Atithi?'

This way. That way. Once I'd ridden up and down every bloody street in a five kilometre-wide radius of the radio station, I knew I was bound to find the hotel eventually. By the time I finally spied the modest sign, I was shattered, and could barely push the bike into the tiny front courtyard.

A hot shower soothed my aching limbs, and against hotel policy, the clerk kindly arranged for room service — hot chips and tomato sauce. Well before nightfall, I crawled into bed. During the day, every vehicle, from trains to trishaws, emits earsplitting blasts on its horn, the louder the better it seems. Not that it makes any difference to the traffic flow. Beeping one's truck horn is an art form in India. But here, in a hotel, the

Ambulance - India

Another rollover - India

silence was almost unnerving.

Next morning I enquired as to where I could get repairs done. 'Yes, good sir,' the obliging desk clerk assured me, 'I know an Indian specialist who can make anything for you, very cheap, very quick. I will send a boy to get him now.'

An amicable fellow duly arrived with tape and chalk, and set about taking measurements. Then he jumped on his bicycle and headed back to his workshop. Here, I thought, is a man who knows his trade. *Wrong!* When he returned an hour later with the new stay, it was 10 centimetres too long. Not to be discouraged, my creative friend measured again, went away, and returned with the replacement in hand. This time it was seven centimetres too short.

It was time to make a suggestion. 'Perhaps I could mark it out on a piece of steel and you cut to my measurements?'

He raised his eyebrows, quizzically, and left, albeit a little less enthusiastically. Nevertheless, he returned with the material. I marked it out, precisely, feeling confident the problem was solved.

The man reappeared with a stay that was more or less like — but not quite the same as — my pattern. This time, though, it did fit. His face lit up. I'm not sure if this was due to relief or pride. Somehow it didn't matter. The lugs he had welded on to fit the mudguard were not at right angles. But that too was a minor technicality, because when I bolted it to the mudguard the lug fell off!

Crestfallen, the engineer took it all off and disappeared again, to re-weld the lugs. This time, they sat three millimetres away from the mudguard. I sensed the man was becoming irritated, and was seeing me as the problem. He asked if he could borrow my file, then sat down on the doorstep of the hotel and filed away for an hour until the surface was flat. Five hours passed before I finally had a rear mudguard stay. Although it didn't look pretty, it did the job, and, in fact, it remained that way until the end of my journey. The price, however, had skyrocketed. I questioned it.

'But, sir, I made you three stays. It is only fair that you pay for them all.' I didn't have the heart to suggest maybe he should be paying me for the engineering lesson. We shook hands. Once again, I put it down to an experience of life on road when you're an old bloke on a bike. And, let's face it, I wasn't paying Australian penalty rates!

Before I left Jaipur I went shopping for sandals. My toes were raw and ugly, and I had to admit my feet were more comfortable without boots. It's just a shame I'm so resistant to doing things that make sense. At least, while I was off the bike, my feet had a chance to heal. But they weren't a pretty sight, which no doubt was unpleasant for the poor shop assistant.

Back in the saddle and beyond the city limits, I faced lashing winds that blew sand stingingly across the road. My arms ached as I fought to keep the motorcycle upright. Despite the conditions, the FN coped reasonably well — until the rear tyre blew out again, the rim gouging into the road. Shit! The low-grade Deestone tyres were proving a nightmare.

By the time I white-knuckled the bike to a halt, my legs were shaking. Several motorists stopped to help and began gathering rocks to jack up the bike.

One man, noticing I had no water, set off, returning half-an-hour later with two full bottles. Meanwhile, his friends had helped me remove the wheel and tyre, ignoring the sandstorm lashing us. Unfortunately, I had only a 19-inch tube, not an easier fitting 21-inch. I hoped it would hold out.

Earlier, in Jaipur, I had spied an advertisement for off-road KTMs, which use the tubes I needed. My excitement was short-lived, the salesman informing me they only intended importing KTM road bikes, whose tubes don't fit my bike.

A few hours after fitting the tyre in the sandstorm, and before I could say goodbye to my good Samaritans and ride to Mangliya Wash, I had to root out my gear, now under a thick layer of sand. I shook everything vigorously, the fine particles having found their way into every nook and cranny. My face felt as though I'd scrubbed it with burnt toast, and my eyes stung. I wiped them on my sleeve and doggedly set off again. A week later, I was still finding sand in pockets and seams.

Construction of an upgraded Jodpur highway meant traffic diversions here and there, creating a vehicular free-for-all. Motorists, impatient at crawling bumper to bumper, drove over footpaths, squeezed into the smallest gaps, and wove around in front of gigantic earthmoving equipment, barely a roti's width between them. I'd had enough, so I staggered in to the next rest stop.

Sweeper - Rajasthan

Tailor - India

Taking in ironing - Rajasthan

8

Cracking up

Lights flashing, horns honking, radios blaring — the truck drivers, oblivious to it all, sat cross-legged on charpoys, engrossed in their steaming mounds of dhal, rice and chapatti, washed down with the obligatory spicy chai.

Between the parking area and the restaurant stood the open-to-the-world shower block. By now, I'd lost all my inhibitions. Much to the amusement of onlookers, I stripped off and ladled ice-cold water over my head. It felt good to remove grit from my eyes and ears and wash away the day's filth. But I did wish I had a larger towel. The one I carried barely covered my bony white arse.

Next morning, I woke to the usual cacophony and smell of spices and diesel. With an early start, I was to cover 160km, but not before I had become lost and frustrated. I wasted an extra 20 kilometres searching for NH112, but my mood lifted briefly when a truck passenger handed down to me a couple of mandarins. No point in being pissed off because I couldn't read instructions.

Valve spring failures happened regularly, and I became adept at sensing the change in sound when something was about to die. Rounding a bend, I saw a railway barrier lowered and a train disappearing from sight. As I slowed gingerly, clutch disengaged, I heard the familiar miss of the engine as a cylinder cut out. Bugger!

When the barrier was raised, I pushed the bike across the tracks and parked against the guardrail. Within minutes, a swarm of people descended, everyone keen to be part of the action. As one tested the horn, another inspected the tools, and, as usual, there was the barrage of questions.

Surprisingly, no one ever said to me, 'Wow, you're riding around the world. Now there's an idea! Can I join you?' Where was their sense of adventure!

Friendly locals - India

Passing the brick pits - India

Despite the circus, I managed to concentrate and put the valve spring back together. My audience gave the bike a push and off I went. But, because of a rough road, I was travelling at the speed of paint drying, and only managed a miserable 53 kilometres for the entire day. I wondered how long the bike could endure the bone-shattering conditions, and questioned if I was as mentally prepared as I'd led myself to believe. Each kilometre was more exhausting than the one before, and although I usually fell into a deep sleep come nighttime, there were times when I would wake with the day's events churning through my head. I'd question my decisions and wrack my brain for solutions to each new problem. The week had been a series of minor mishaps. Seems I was saving the big ones for later.

I thought about how I had once considered moving the bike across India by train. I'd read in the 46-page *Indian Railway Claims Manual* that motorcycles had to be 'tightly wrapped in straw, sewn in sacking and manually lifted' onto trains. I could see all sorts of problems arising from that practice, especially if the back wheel accidently turned and the engine started.

And there were a few gems in the manual, for example, the statement that 'bidis' (cheap Indian cigarettes) had to be contained in bitumised waterproof paper. Surely that didn't include the old biddies that live next door!

And another: 'Raw liver must be placed in a plastic bag and packed in ice in a wooden case with a conical wooden lid. The lid will prevent the case from being turned upside down, and avoid pilferage.'

It troubled me that, if raw liver was in danger of being knocked off, an old motorcycle could also be pretty tempting. Given that the extent of the railways responsibility for a motorcycle is only one percent of its declared value — while for an elephant it is Rp 60000 — I opted to ride the FN across India while Lynne took the train.

Thankfully, Hotel Devi Bhawan, the accommodation at Jodphur, was easy to find. There, with Lynne, for the next three nights, I was able to unwind and recover from the gruelling challenge of keeping the bike and myself going.

Rakesh, the manager, kindly pointed me in the right direction of an aged upholsterer, who had a face like a crumpled paper bag and a disarming toothless grin. He was happy to make a new seat for the bike, the original having grown increasingly uncomfortable. His vinyl creation, with ample padding, was not a work of art, but it was fit for the job.

The next task was to find an engineering shop where the crown wheel and brake drum could be unscrewed to replace broken spokes. I would love to have found a quiet corner to work unhindered, but the reality was that I was a curiosity and an audience was inevitable.

Before leaving Jodhpur I washed the panniers, cleaned my gear, stocked up on oil, and checked and tightened every nut and bolt. Devi Bhawan staff gave me a hearty send-off as I began what turned out to be a monotonous ride through a dry desert landscape.

I'd been told the road was sealed all the way, and I managed to cover 200 kilometres in good time. Then, just before Bikaner, the highway turned into a minefield of potholes. Just keeping the bike upright was a battle as I bashed and crashed my way over the lunar landscape. Then the pannier straps broke and the bike fell over. I could count on one hand the number of times I've fallen off the FN. This time, it was simply fatigue that saw me laying in the dirt and cursing the dreadful conditions. The mirror broke, the pedal was destroyed, and the pedal crank was bent.

I desperately needed a 15-inch crescent spanner to straighten the crank, but I didn't have one with me and most garages had only a few basic tools. There's usually no shortage of bicycle repair shops in India, but I had trouble finding one in Bikaner. When I did, I arrived pushing the bike with a throng trailing behind me. I must have looked like the Pied Piper.

The hyperactive manner of the wiry little owner was unnerving to say the least. But he was the only one in town with a Stillson wrench big enough to straighten the pedal crank. He replaced the right-hand pedal, but refused to replace the other.

'If I sell you the last one, then I won't have anything for my next customer,' he rationalised.

This cracked me up. I understood his sentiments, but it didn't help that I now had mismatched pedals. The luggage straps would have to wait until I reached a bigger city. For now, all I could do was reposition the load. A new Indian mirror replaced my broken one and would suffice until I could have new glass fitted.

The only highlight of my day was a haircut and shave at a tiny stall, with one plastic chair, in the middle of nowhere. Not surprisingly, a crowd materialised.

That evening, the manager of Tata Trucks provided a room for me next to his workshop. Before bed, I woofed down a meal of stuffed tomatoes, dhal, rotis and a bottle of cola. All-up cost: 125 rupees (about 25 cents Australian).

First blown tyre - India

Leaving the hotel - Jodhpur

When Lynne and I talked each night via Skype, I'd relay entries from my diary. Fortunately Lynne's laptop had reasonable internet connection most of the time. Phone cards are cheap and easily procurable throughout India. Even the poorest people I met had mobile phones, some several, which enabled them to take advantage of cheaper rates at different times.

'How's your day been?' Lynne asked. I told her how pissed off I was at dropping the bike. And that the Dry Rider gear bags weren't holding up as well as I expected. She shared my sentiments and asked if I was okay.

'I'm fine. I just put a hole in my jacket. In fairness, the bags are under a lot of stress and are probably are carrying more than the recommended five kilos. The problem is that I need to carry extra fuel, and that's so damned heavy. What gets me most is that I was told the road was good, but it turned out to be crap most of the way. It's always like this: I get told one thing and it proves to be another, and the heavy load doesn't help.'

Whenever I share my frustrations, things don't seem quite as dire.

We discussed the alternatives, but I already knew the answer. Going back wasn't an option; neither was having a backup team. Tomorrow was bound to be better — well surely it couldn't get worse!

Street food - India

Crowded streets - Jodhpur

9

Pushing the Boundaries

If I had bet that conditions would take a turn for the better, I'd have lost big time. On the road to Ganganagar, I spent nearly two hours covering the first 15 kilometres of broken, cambered asphalt. Following trucks wiggling their way through the maze of potholes made it even more difficult for me to decide which path to take. All the ducking and diving flung my backpack from one side to another, making it difficult to balance the FN. Because of the bike's height, I found it hard to get my foot down quickly to stabilise the machine. Continuously adjusting the backpack made keeping my hands on the handlebars impossible. My shoulders ached from the constant jarring, each jolt threatening to throw me. Gaping holes on every bridge I crossed added to challenge. Just when I began to think I couldn't go any further, conditions did eventually improve.

I pulled into a fuel stop to rest, and while I checked the spokes and tensioned bolts, the owner made me a cup of tea. I admired his embroidered leather slippers.

'My aunty brought them back from Iran,' he said proudly. Toes upturned, the shoes looked straight out of the Arabian Nights. I wondered if I was ever going to make it to Iran — a country so far away.

I pressed on, but when the night chill settled in sooner than I expected I pulled into a dhaba for a hot meal. A freezing shower left my teeth chattering, so I gratefully accepted a couple of dusty, ragged blankets from the proprietor before crawling into my sleeping bag.

Next morning, the bike wouldn't start, constant tampering by curious fingers having pulled the nipple off the throttle cable. Luckily, I had a solderless nipple that could be attached with a screwdriver.

I could understand people's curiosity, but it was wearing on me to have to ask everyone not to touch the bike's fragile components. Even back home, 'Don't touch' signs usually don't work because people simply can't help themselves.

The strong rubber band I had used on the brake lever — to stop the brake from being engaged when the machine was pushed backwards — had perished. When I couldn't find a replacement, I fashioned a clip that restricted the throttle from opening fully.

Another problem was my right toe. The infection had intensified and was causing me great pain. Whenever I halted, I removed my boots to ease the throbbing. And then I cringed and had to grit my teeth when I put them on again. Riding in sandals was not an option: It was better to lose one digit through infection than a whole foot through stupidity.

When a young bystander insisted on taking me to a doctor, I consented. I left the bike at a café and hobbled down a back alley, the boy holding my elbow.

'This way, Uncle,' he said, leading me into the surgery.

The tiny bare room was clean and bright. I removed my sandal and the kindly doctor set a kidney bowl under my foot. I grimaced as he cleaned away the oozing pus. He dabbed the toe with peroxide, covered it in iodine cream, and then bandaged the foot firmly.

When I took out my wallet, he waved his hand and frowned: 'No, you are a guest in my country. Please have a safe journey.'

A few days later, the youngster phoned to check I was okay, and to make sure I had changed the dressings as instructed. Next day, he called again, and the next. This concern for a total stranger was extremely touching, and typical of so many I met along the way.

I was still losing weight. Obviously, I wasn't eating enough to counter my physical exertions. I became so focused on the FN and what I needed to do to keep it going that I neglected to take care of myself. When I forced myself to eat and drink well, it made a noticeable difference to how I coped.

Early on, when I often skipped meals, I found myself tiring early and losing patience more quickly. I tried to follow a routine that involved starting the day with a good breakfast, eating plenty of fruit along the way, and ensuring that I had at least one hot meal a day. I also tried to set up camp before becoming worn out, take a shower as often as possible, and listen to my body. Sometimes, though, the unpredictability of life on the road meant all this went out the window.

It wasn't always easy to end a day's travel where accommodation was available, or to find a meal when I felt hungry. Nor was it easy to avoid stress. But I always tried. Only when I was with Lynne did I get a varied diet. Unable to cook or carry fresh food, I was relying largely on local fare. Fortunately, I've never been picky, even when faced with the unfamiliar. As long a meal was piping hot, I tried not to worry about how it had been prepared. I should have made a greater effort to eat more, but fatigue frequently got the better of my good intentions.

Remaining cheerful under pressure was sometimes difficult. I sang and whistled often. My rendition of 'Me and Bobbie McGee' and 'Starry, Starry Night' might not have been recognisable to locals, but they made me smile and lifted my spirits, especially when I felt weary. Now and then I had a conversation with the little voice in my head, and, if I got lonely, I talked to the bike. Mostly, I enjoyed meeting people and sharing my experiences, even though it did mean recounting a story a million times. I reassured myself that everyone was hearing my story only once, so it was important not to become jaded by the repetitiveness of it all.

I had to try to avoid risks and not tempt luck — yet some risks were unavoidable. Riding after dark was a definite no-no, but there were times when something had gone awry, and I found myself pressing on further than I intended because I was unsure if I'd find a place to stay.

Although I will sometimes put my own safety and health at risk, throughout the journey I was always vigilant about the welfare and upkeep of the FN. Given her age, I was asking of her far more than was reasonable, so being constantly on the alert for problems was vital.

An important factor in my Nepal-Belgium odyssey was that, for most of the journey I had no set timetable or agenda. Thus I was able to take each day as it came. I simply kept reminding myself that, 'There will be good days and bad days'. At Ganganagar, I was telling myself that, if I could stave off a major infection in my toe, eat more, remain optimistic, be vigilant, and take good care of the bike I stood a reasonable chance of survival. That, I felt, wasn't too much to ask. Or was it?

Moghul Fort - Rajasthan

Rajasthan - India

10

Music to My Ears

A constant rhythm told me all was well. If the sound changed, even slightly, I would adjust the throttle/air lever to avoid contamination in carburettor jet. If the engine failed to respond, or hiccupped, I knew the inlet-valve spring was collapsing. I could gauge how much lubrication the engine was getting by the amount of oil flecks on my right boot. And, the amount of oil from the clutch that appeared on my left boot within the first five or six kilometres depended on how often I used it.

When I applied the back brakes using the pedals, this put pressure on the brake pawl. Basically a ratchet for the pedaling device, the pawl soon wore out with the constant braking, mainly as I negotiated my way through towns. I carried a spare pawl and, when necessary, had the old one welded. It was too scary to contemplate having to apply the brake in horrendous city traffic and finding it wasn't working. Mostly, I used the decompressor to try to slow the engine.

The first time this happened I was cruising down a long hill. Alarmingly, I felt no resistance when I applied the brake. Every muscle tensed. Nothing was happening.

Ahead, the traffic had stopped. But I was past the point of no return and, shaking my head in disbelief, found myself weaving erratically along the nearside of the parked vehicles, all the while beeping the horn. Eventually, having managed to dodge everything, I brought the bike to a standstill. Heartbeat thrashing in my ears, I dragged it onto the footpath.

Once I got my breath back, it took 15 minutes to work out why the brake had failed. I tried turning the back brake, and discovered the problem was the pawl. It was only a five-minute job to replace it.

Each time I took a break from riding, I drained the oil from the distributor that had seeped through from the camshaft spindle in the timing case. A proper seal had worked well, but unfortunately it hadn't lasted. Now I had to turn off the oil whenever I stopped for an extended period. Come the end of the day, I had dismantled and adjusted every one of the inlet-valve springs. The short rides in Australia had failed to show up the problems I was to run into and I went through a real learning curve in those first weeks after leaving Kathmandu.

The difficulty of putting down the rear stand, because of the amount of luggage strapped on, usually meant parking the motorcycle against a post. Before hitting the sack each night, I needed to drain and clean the carburettor jet; and, before starting next morning, check that I had 45 PSI in the back tyre. This way, I knew the bike and I stood a good chance of a relatively trouble-free day. No guarantees, mind you, but the routine did give me peace of mind. Every night, I wiped over the bike, not just to give it a clean, but to alert me to anything that might be working loose. I'm sure the little machine appreciated being cared for.

Riding the bike while searching for anything was a nightmare. So, at Ganganagar, I walked many miles to find a shop where I could get the mirror repaired. When I at last found one, I supplied a perfect cardboard template. With all the usual Indian enthusiasm, the man told me to come back in an hour.

The new mirror looked okay, but, on closer inspection, I noticed it had a 10-millimetre band of brown sealant all around the rim. Cutting it back, I discovered the diameter of the glass was 20 millimetres too small. I removed the rest of the sealant and the obliging man tried again. He was to cut four pieces of glass before finally getting it right. This time I wasn't asked to pay for the rejects!

I received a message on my mobile that the authorisation number for my Iran visa had finally arrived, which meant I could collect it in Lahore. This was a relief. I didn't fancy the alternative of trying to find another route to Turkey that might mean even more pushing of the bike.

Lynne and I had arranged to meet in Amritsar on March 4 to spend a few days together before I crossed into Pakistan. Though nearly the end of February, I was optimistic I'd cover the distance from Ganganagar to Amritsar in ample time. But today I wasn't feeling too good.

So far, I'd been lucky not to acquire 'Delhi belly' and the shop signs: JOLLY FAT GO, LIVE KEBABS, and PISSA didn't instill much confidence. What I craved was something cold and fizzy to settle my stomach. With people coughing all around me, maybe I should have been more concerned about contracting tuberculosis than diarrhoea. There

Golden Palace - Amritsar

Morning light - Udaipur

were only so many issues I could fret about! Despite the nausea and mild cramping, I managed to swing a leg over the bike and get going.

I'd been trying to locate the NH15 for some time, but could only find NH10 and 20. Exasperated, I pulled into a gas station. The owner sat me down, brought a cup of sweet tea, then instructed a worker to take his motorcycle and guide me through the town and back 10 kilometres to the main road.

A little later, I stopped when I saw a sign, on the side of a building, for Airtel. It turned out not to be a shop selling phone cards, as I had hoped, the sign being simply Airtel advertising. But my stop was not entirely in vain. When it turned out that the owner's daughter lived in Brisbane, he dashed to the phone to tell her that a man from Queensland was in his store.

Although it was the middle of the night in Australia, I was invited to exchange a few pleasantries with Rosa. She was extremely polite, and insisted her family give me all the support I needed. Without hesitation, her father urged his son to take me on his motorcycle to a phone shop. Something must have been missing from our conversation because, once I had my phone card, the boy then took me to the bus station.

'Off here for the bus, Uncle,' he said, proudly showing off his English. I had to explain I needed to go back to my bike and get back on the road to Amritsar.

By the time I reached my next planned stop, my stomach had settled. There, I accepted an invitation by the owners of the small dhaba to spend the night in their house rather than outdoors. Over a dinner of delicious egg-and-vegetable pastie, I discovered they had a son living in Victoria. What a small world it was proving to be!

All big Indian cities were a nightmare for me on arrival, and Amritsar was no exception. I was looking for the Golden Tulip Hotel, and I knew it was on a main road, but no one I spoke to could tell me where it was. Eventually, I discovered that the Golden Tulip had undergone a name change in recent years but the locals still knew it by its old name.

In stop-start traffic, with oil pouring from the clutch, the bike overheated. Eventually, FN and I, both ready to erupt, reeled in through the entrance of the rather opulent hotel. A turbaned doorman, after greeting us, directed me to the underground carpark where I could store the bike.

In the lobby I caught a glimpse of my reflection and cringed: what must the engaging hotel manager have thought of my appearance? If he noted I wasn't four-star clientele, his face didn't show it. It turned out he was an avid biker, and, like everyone else at the hotel, was welcoming and courteous.

Upstairs in my room, I slipped into a steaming bath, tipped my head back, and closed my eyes. At last I could escape from the maddening traffic.

Later, wrapped in a fresh white bath towel, I bundled my filthy kit into a laundry bag, embarrassed by the riding gear caked in grime and oh so smelly socks! Next morning, the lot was returned, dry-cleaned and freshly pressed.

Lynne soon joined me, after spending the week in Udaipur, and set about editing our photographs, now numbering hundreds. Our separate journeys were poles apart. Her pictures captured the essence of daily life in the Lake City: women bathing at the ghats; the milk vendor rugged up in a beanie and blanket, pouring liquid from a brass churn; and a machinist seated at her treadle machine in a narrow doorway.

Unfortunately, I did not have the luxury of waiting for the perfect lighting or composition. When I did stop to take photographs, attention was immediately drawn to the FN and the moment was lost.

Over dinner, Lynne recounted her experience with a masseur in Udaipur. A masseur? I could have done with one of those!

Each morning Lynne was greeted by a lean, bespectacled man; his graying ponytail pulled back from a nut-brown face. Raju stood outside his shop inviting passing tourists in for breakfast or Ayurvedic treatment. With a mix of guile and Eastern charm, he and Ansh, his handsome son, expressed their admiration for all things Australian, French or Swiss, depending on where each tourist hailed from.

Despite her niggling aches and pains, Lynne repeatedly turned down the invitation. But, on her last day in Udaipur, she said she capitulated, and followed the masseur up a narrow staircase and into a room smaller than a shoebox. While she slipped off her outer garments, Raju stripped down to a loincloth, insistent he needed freedom to move.

'You must relax,' he urged, oiling his hands and climbing astride her back. 'I can feel all your tension.' While he alleviated the pain in her legs, albeit temporarily, some of the man's techniques seemed a little unorthodox to Lynne. He was adamant that her body was out of alignment, and extra time was needed to put things right.

With some deft manipulation, Raju claimed to have solved the problem, and moved on to treating other so-called 'ailments'.

Haircut - India

Rest stop Jaipur - India

'When his hands began wandering up my legs like a bloody spider, I thought it was definitely time to call it quits,' Lynne told me. After sharing her experience, the jury remained out on whether the man was a healer or a charlatan. Lynne thought that at her age she should know the difference. Fortunately, we were able to see the humor in the situation. This was India after all, where one can always expect the unexpected.

In Amritsar, I found a tailor to mend the burn holes in my pants and reinforce the panniers. I also braved the streets in search of a couple of spare distributor brushes. The speed at which they were wearing out was worrying. I tried in vain to buy a new brass horn, the one on the bike having had the life squeezed out of it by enthusiastic admirers. It seemed that, though there were brass milk cans all over Amritsar, there were no brass horns to be found. This was a bit strange given replica horns for sale in Australia and elsewhere are mostly made in India.

At the Golden Tulip, Lynne and I worked to bring the blog up to date. Judicious editing of my daily journal, we hoped, would make for enjoyable reading by friends and followers of the FN trail. It was always fun for us to be together again, and a reminder of how much we enjoyed each other's company.

I raised the idea of Lynne joining me in Pakistan and Iran. At first, my suggestion met with little enthusiasm. 'There's no way I'm wearing a hijab,' she grimaced.

I understood her reticence. Being covered from head to foot wasn't exactly an appealing proposition, especially in the heat. And, there was the question of how a Western woman, traveling alone, might be viewed in Muslim society.

But our random meetings were cherished. They provided me with a release and helped put things into perspective. I would be sorry to see her leave. Being on my own worked well when I was riding, and I enjoyed the fact that it afforded me the opportunity to experience aspects of every-day-life that few others got to see. But, there was so much we could share and I would be disappointed if she didn't at least consider the suggestion.

Later, after reading glowing online accounts by women who'd travelled through the Middle East, Lynne began to warm to the idea. Despite having to comply with the strict dress codes, Westerners invariably find Iran a fascinating country and Iranians extremely hospitable. There was less information about travelling in Pakistan, but, as it was only necessary for her to go to Lahore to collect an Iranian visa, she wasn't fazed.

Once Lynne decided she would travel to Pakistan, and then join me later in Iran, we went in search of a shop specialising in shalwar kameez: baggy pants and long shirt, and dupatta, a matching scarf. With hundreds of glittering fabrics and colours to choose from, Lynne settled on something that wouldn't make her too conspicuous. The tailor promised to sew and deliver two outfits to our hotel by 9.00 pm that evening.

With a mixture of excitement and apprehension, Lynne and I made final preparations for my crossing into Pakistan. We knew little about the country other than how it was portrayed by the media, but we have always been eager to get to places less travelled. When I was crossing the border, Lynne would be on her way back to Australia to arrange her visas and fulfil a housesitting commitment. Then she would fly back to Pakistan.

On our last day in Amritsar, we visited the Golden Temple, a significant place of Sikh worship. In stark contrast to the madness of the dusty streets outside, the Golden Temple proved a dazzling spectacle.

When I was waiting for the panniers straps to be reinforced, I witnessed a nasty motorcycle accident. With no ambulance available, the injured man was tossed into the back of a rickshaw with little concern that he might be suffering head trauma or spinal injury. His journey to hospital would have been a slow one. It was a sobering reminder that, should I have an accident, specialised medical care was not likely to be available outside major cities.

I said goodbye to Lynne next morning, mindful it would be some weeks before we saw each other again. The accident the day before had shaken me up more than I cared to admit, with the image of the broken and bleeding motorcyclist still fresh in my mind. But there was nothing I could do to change whatever fate had in store. Best not to dwell on such things!

Border crossing - India

Border crossing - India

11

The Best Laid Plans

By the time I reached the border with Pakistan, via the Grand Trunk Road, trucks overloaded with potatoes and onions queued back three kilometres. Even though the Attari customs and migration office supposedly opened at 8.00 am, nothing happened until about two hours later — and even then it took customs officers ages to find the cumbersome ledger that deals with people like me.

A long drawn-out ticking of boxes and stamping of the carnet began. Each time the clerk had to attend another busload of transit passengers, he'd forget where he left off with my paperwork. Five migration officers checked my passport, I think purely out of curiosity; and, of course, everyone, even the bus passengers, had to inspect the bike and have their photo taken with it. It was all par for the course.

'Australians are hardworking. Indians are hardly working,' joked one Indian customs agent. I didn't have the heart to ruin his joke by telling him this just wasn't true. Finally, at 11.30, I got the all clear.

As I was about to push the FN across the 100 metres of no-man's land between the border posts, I thought about how much I had enjoyed India. Before leaving home, I'd heard conflicting stories about the country: some people loved it with a passion and others found it tested them to the extreme. Me? I had warmed to India. Sure, there were day-to-day challenges that became frustrating, but most were not entirely unexpected. The crowds for instance. Heaven knows I experienced them regularly in the 1980s when we travelled through South America. There were times then when the police urged us to move on as quickly as possible because we were causing traffic chaos, with hundreds of locals rubber-necking for a look at the bike.

That journey was luxurious in comparison to the one I was now on:

padded leather seats, air suspension, a reliable machine that could handle almost everything we threw at it, and a trailer carrying all mod cons. We carried detailed maps, and Lynne gave directions to me over our intercom. Now, I was responsible for everything, and at times, when I was too tired to think straight, it became overwhelming. But, to tell the truth, this would have applied wherever I was. Even Sydney at rush hour can be a nightmare, and there are no tuk-tuks or camel-carts sharing the road there!

When I stopped for a few days, showered, slept in a decent bed, and ate well, my energy levels rose. I could take in the sights and truly relax. But these days were few and far between. I had limited time in which to reach Europe. Riding the FN would be impossible once the monsoon season arrived on the Indian subcontinent or in Western Asia.

Despite the eternal exhaust fumes that made my eyes water and throat rasp, the frustration of doing cross-cultural business, and navigating crushing throngs, on bike and foot, I found much about the country to love: the warmth and generosity of all those I'd met; the brilliant costumes amid dust, pollution and chaos; the splendid monuments; the dogged resilience of people living constantly in the face of adversity...

Inevitably, on a journey like this, some things have to be endured rather than appreciated. I knew I would be back to visit India again one day to fully enjoy all she had to offer. For now though, I had experienced the country in way few others do, and despite the drawbacks, the experience had been priceless.

If India was a pointer, I had a feeling Pakistan was going to surprise me even more. I knew it was here in these border regions in 1947 that the bloodshed of partition and the exodus of millions occurred. I wondered how it must have been for all those who had been displaced.

At sundown each day, between Attari and Wagah, Indian and Pakistani military perform the Beating the Retreat ceremony with intense nationalistic fervour. I was told it was an impressive spectacle but, keen to get going, I had no intention of hanging about until 6.00 pm.

On the Wagah side of the border, the power was cut. Friendly officials insisted the bike be wheeled inside, probably more out of their curiosity than for any good reason. As they ogled the machine, everyone from the highest-ranking officer to the porters posed for pictures. Meanwhile, I sipped through several cups of tea. Five hours later, power was restored and my paperwork was swiftly sorted.

I'd been told a group of Pakistani bikers would meet me at the border, but it seemed there'd been a miscommunication. When no one appeared I called Omar, a member of the Pakistani Biker's Club. Armed with an address, I headed for Lahore, totally unprepared for the huge modern ring-road system that lay ahead.

A non-English-speaking mini-cab driver, waving away my willingness to pay, offered to lead me. Without his help, I can only imagine how difficult it could have been to find my way. The roads were wider, cleaner and in better condition than anything I'd been on in recent weeks.

Omar and his wife, Asma, made me welcome in their home, and they lent me a little Suzuki motorcycle to get around town. Club members arrived to inspect the FN. In those parts, a machine so old would have been a rare sight indeed.

Next day, Zaca, the club's president, an impressive looking man with a huge mustache, took me to the Iranian embassy. The complicated visa procedure involved several trips back and forth across the city over several days. The first day, I arrived at 8.30 am, filled out the forms and sat and waited for an hour. When my turn came, I was told to get a short-term visa at the border then extend it in the first large town I came to. I explained that the visa number for the required period had already been issued, in Australia. So then they instructed me to return next day, at 4.30 pm. This turned out to be prayer day, Friday, so I had to wait until Saturday.

I spent most of Friday with television crews from various channels. Questions and answers flew back and forth for nearly five hours, everyone polite and enthusiastic. When I had a spare moment, I went in search of bike spokes. No luck. I'd seen the correct size on Omar's '76 Honda XL, but what I needed wasn't available in Lahore. Omar promised to buy some from Karachi as soon as he could.

At the Iranian embassy next morning, I waited until 10.30 before being directed to an interview room. An hour later, in another room, they opened a huge ledger to check my name against their numbers. Lo and behold, there it was! With a slip of paper in hand, I was sent downstairs to pay a fee, only to be informed when I got there, that the cashier's office was closed for the day. I had to leave my passport there with $US100 and return on Monday to pick up the visa. Despite all the frustrations, the staff always treated me with great courtesy. It was all happening at a snail's pace, but at least I was moving forward.

About 25 biker club members gathered in a park on the weekend to raise motorcycle-safety awareness. A large crowd attended, and many, young and old, paid a lot of attention to the FN. One lovely gesture, among many, came from a woman who apologised for not having a gift for me — so she bought me an ice cream instead.

The FN and I appeared on television across the nation. It wasn't surprising therefore, that from then on I was often recognised. People everywhere wanted to shake my hand. I found it strange to be treated like a celebrity, but understood people's fascination with what I was doing.

At night, Omar took me on a street crawl of some of his favourite eateries. Among regional delicacies we savoured bulls' balls. Omar used a novel way of paying the bills: he would buy a phone-card for a specific amount, tell the retailer the scratch number to install on his phone, and everything was square. I'd never seen anything like it before.

Ali and Akbar, two biker club members took me on a grand tour of the Shahi Qila Fort and Badshahi mosque. We drove to the Old City, again savoring a range of local foods. I arrived home at midnight so stuffed I didn't think I'd eat again for a week.

A club member observed that the FN's front wheel was wobbling. As the bearing was 30 years old, it wasn't surprising that the grease in it had well and truly dried out. This, plus rough roads, had caused it to collapse. A new one had to be machined. I was carrying two spares, but these were larger on the outside diameter than those in the wheel, as they were all I could buy at the time. I would need to have them machined to fit the hub. Anyone in their right mind would have had this done before they left home!

Ali and Akbar escorted me to the United Engineering Company shop to have the bearings machined. Production on one of their machines was halted to accommodate me, but work had hardly begun when the power went down. A generator was started up, and they ground the outside diameters to my specifications. The whole process took one-and-a-half hours.

Assembly of the front bearing went without a hitch, and, when it was done, I went in search of a shop to buy a few more bearings. Having too many was better than not enough. Logic dictates I should have visited the bearing shop first, so a spare set could be machined simultaneously, but I wasn't expecting to have to replace the bearings again any time soon. This would prove to be my undoing.

When I took off my crash helmet, the bearing supplier exclaimed, 'I saw you on television!' and insisted I would get one bearing free because he was so honoured that I'd chosen his shop. The truth is, I couldn't find another shop that sold bearings, and I happily paid for three more. The

News report - Pakistan

One of many television interviews - Lahore, Pakistan

Everyone wants a look - Pakistan

kindnesses I was receiving were to prove typical of Pakistani hospitality.

For the next two hours I wandered through the UNESCO World Heritage Shalimar Gardens, before returning to the Iranian embassy to collect my visa. But Monday, it turned out, was a holiday, so that meant yet another day's delay. By Tuesday, I was free to explore Pakistan.

I had long wanted to travel the Karakoram Highway, but riding the FN on the KKH, as it is commonly known, would take weeks out of my schedule, and besides, the conditions were notoriously rough. So I left the bike in Omar's care. What a wise decision that proved to be! I also gave the spokes to Ali and Akbar to be cut to length and threaded as per my instructions.

I decided to take the bus to Gilgit rather than fly because aircraft are frequently turned back in poor weather. My plan was to hire a small motorcycle and explore the border area, so I took my helmet along just in case I had the opportunity to ride.

Ali arrived at 5.30 am to drive me to the bus station for the first leg to Islamabad. I was pleased to be boarding a modern private Daiwoo coach, with a professional driver, for the three-hour journey. However, when the bus arrived at the Islamabad depot, my hopes that the same degree of comfort would continue were soon dashed. As they say, the best laid plans…

Farewell to friends in Lahore - Pakistan

Lahore mosque - Pakistan

12

The Karakoram

The government bus to Gilgit — inaptly named the 'VIP Express' — was an hour late. Not a good start.

All day long we rattled through a monochromatic, rocky landscape, the horizon now and then jagged by snow-tipped peaks. Through areas considered dangerous, traffic drove in convoys, escorted by the military. Punctures and frequent passport and identity checks slowed our journey. Our first driver stayed at the wheel 14 hours. When he finally stumbled to the back for a sleep, his replacement cranked up the pace, overtaking everything in his path, often on blind bends.

After dark, too nervous to sleep, I stared bug-eyed into the void. I was relieved to no longer be able to see the drop-offs spilling hundreds of feet to the river below, but glimpses of the twisting, unsealed road in the headlights was still unnerving. What should have been a 24-hour journey had dragged into 32. Unsteady, and barely coherent, I staggered off the bus and into the North Inn. Once highly rated, the hotel now had a distinct air of neglect. My room, though windowless and scantily furnished, was clean, and it had hot water — well, at least initially. Ignoring the traffic noise and chatter outside, I buried my head beneath the blankets and slept until the next morning.

Still feeling the effects of that harrowing bus drive, I tried without luck, to hire a motorcycle. Dammit, I'd carried the helmet for nothing.

Raja, the owner of the local internet café, downloaded my photos on his old PC, and dispatched them to Lynne. I was grateful for his patience. Frequent power outages forced him to use a small stand-by generator, dragging the download process on for hours.

Gilgit, once an important city on the Silk Road, is a major hub for summer treks and Himalayan mountaineering expeditions. At this time

Rockslide, Karakoram Highway - Pakistan

Another meal of chicken & rice - Pakistan

Hamburger stop - Pakistan

of year, it was little more than a lively, yet, dusty bazaar. A heavy armed police and military presence has become every-day normality, which is a little disconcerting, though understandable, given a recent history of terrorist insurgency.

Omar had suggested visiting Hunza, 100 kilometres north, near the Chinese border. Now that I was this far, I figured I might as well press on.

While I waited for a bus, I went in search of a tailor's shop. There, an elderly man hunched over a treadle sewing machine, and in the dim light did his best to mend a hole in my jacket. The bright green cotton he used stood out like a sore thumb, but it did the job.

Two hours later, I was on my way. Though the sealed road deteriorated the farther we travelled, it was heaven compared to my Karakoram experience.

Late in the afternoon, we pulled into an open market. Freshly killed animals hung from meathooks, among assorted vegetables, pots, pans and other household goods.

I inspected take-away food stalls. 'These are really bad for you,' one guy joshed, gesturing toward a batch of pasties he had just taken from a brick oven. I took my chances. Goodness knows what meat was in them, but those pasties were juicy and delicious.

It was close to midnight by the time we reached Hunza. The temperature had plummeted to one below zero and it had snowed a few days before. The tourist season didn't start for another month, so hotels were not prepared for visitors. After repeated knocks on the door of the Hotel Kariabad Zero Point, a man finally appeared, candle in hand, and ushered me in. Upstairs, the kitchen fire and a cup of green tea warmed me a little.

My room was damp and musty and I sat with my feet in a bucket of hot water until they thawed. Exhausted, I crawled into bed, shivering under a layer of heavy quilts until sleep descended.

The owner briefed me over breakfast. Between May and October, he said, when the valley comes alive with blossoms, tourists pour in to enjoy the scenery: motorcycling, fishing, trekking and paragliding. Although it was only March, and buds were just appearing on the walnut trees, spring was a long way off. Still, I decided to spend a few days exploring.

At an altitude of 2,438 metres, Hunza is surrounded by some of the most spectacular peaks in the world, several rising to more than 6,000 metres. The bounty of the valley includes apples, apricots, cherries, peaches, walnuts, almonds, mulberries, pears and grapes.

In 2010, a huge landslide blocked 27 kilometres of the Karakoram Highway and threatened the safety of 15,000 people in the valley below. The Attabad Lake was created when the same landslide effectively blocked off the Hunza River. These avalanches occur often, especially when explosives are detonated in the search of gold. When I sat out on the hotel terrace it was unnerving to suddenly hear an immense boom, feel the earth shake, then see a mass of loosened rock, snow and ice cascade down the mountainside across the river.

On the first day, I walked for hours, taking in all the sights: ancient petroglyphs, huge brick kilns, neatly tended fields, the Baltit Fort, the daubed-stone animal shelters… On my return, as I walked above the swift flowing river, police — who'd been sound asleep when I crossed earlier in the day — warned me not to take photos of the checkpoint or bridge. So much for security! I sat in the tiny outpost and sipped tea, while the two officers quizzed me about my travels.

Still etched in my mind was the road journey I had endured to get to Gilgit. Flying there would have been a spectacular, and a preferable option. And my return journey was still ahead! What should I do?

I considered travelling east, on to Skardu, to visit the seven-storey Kharphocho Fort, dating from the eighth century. But, it seemed there wasn't a direct route to get there, and no one in Hunza could tell me where to rent a small motorcycle. Also, everyone insisted Skardu was even more unsettled and better to avoid. I took the hint. Before leaving for Gilgit, I decided to give my spare headlamp to my host to help him through the frequent power outages.

It was not long after leaving Hunza that our bus had a flat tyre, forcing another long delay. The spare was in far worse condition than the flat one, so we limped carefully on to the next repair shop, where the driver was able to buy a secondhand tyre, only half as worn.

Back at the North Inn Hotel in Gilgit, I suffered gripping cramp. I took a handful of pills and hoped for the best. Next day, I had recovered sufficiently to walk the two kilometres to the airport to see if I could get a flight back to Lahore. With loose bowels, I was fearful of retracing the Karakoram Highway, so I desperately needed another way out.

Poor visibility meant no planes had arrived or left for a week, and bad weather was forecast for the next two days. From the hotel, I had heard the sound of aircraft engines, and could see people excitedly surging toward the airport. False alarm: although planes were taxi-ing up and

Views from bus, Karakoram Highway - Pakistan

Local transport - Gilgit, Pakistan

down the runway, someone would always appear to announce, 'Not today. Insha'Allah, (God willing), tomorrow.'

Things were not looking good and the bus was my only option. When I turned up at the bus depot, it had been raining for 24 hours. Chaos reigned: horns blaring, people shouting, children crying, luggage being thrown around, vehicles being directed in and out, everyone scrambling aboard buses with enough food to see them back to Islamabad.

The bus was late leaving. An hour into the journey it ended at a huge rockslide that had completely blocked the road. Passengers made valiant efforts to clear enough room for the bus to pass, but the job was impossible without bulldozers. It was back to Gilgit.

Next day, no buses were leaving, and no one knew when the road would be open. Again I walked to the airport, just in time to see a plane taking off: I'd missed the day's only flight. Bugger.

Two days later, on another bus, and again after only an hour, we found the KKH blocked, but in a different place. Drivers of the five buses held up decided on a detour, and we set off in convoy, passing through small villages and crossing narrow suspension bridges. At each bridge, the passengers had to get out, because the drivers insisted it wouldn't carry their weight.

Once through the detour and back on the KKH, we were stopped regularly at police checks. As the only foreigner, I was removed from the bus each time to fill in passport details. Each time I clambered back on board I was met with scowls from other passengers who resented the delays I was causing.

Due to the possibility of insurgents in the area, the police accompanied us for four hours over about 60 kilometres. I was more afraid of overhanging rocks that could fall and crush us. A month later, I learned that my nervousness was justified. One hundred-and-thirty Pakistani soldiers on patrol had been buried under an avalanche northeast of Gilgit. It was a sobering reminder of the region's instability.

At times, the Karakoram petered out into a one-lane muddy track, almost impossible to negotiate. At 4.00 pm, the bus ground to a halt. Rocks were piled in our path. This time bulldozers were working to clear the mess. Before long we were bumping and grinding through the rubble.

By now, the journey was taking its toll on our driver. His gear changes had become so slow the engine threatened to stall. No one else seemed concerned when I had to shake him awake. It might have been because they were all asleep themselves — or perhaps they just didn't care. Insha'Allah!

After 24 hours of stop-start travel, our bus lurched into the national capital. As I got out of the bus, an impromptu backyard band was hammering in my head. I could still feel the seat springs grinding into my derriere and my limbs were stiff and aching. Trying to get my bearings, I had to decide which way to go. That's when I noticed a message on my mobile.

While I'd been enjoying a drive to hell and back, Lynne had been in touch with a blog follower who had sent an email offering me somewhere to stay in Islamabad. I couldn't contain my surprise when I called the number and found Enum was a young woman!

I took a taxi to her home, where I met her dad, Noor, who was ex-military, and her mum, Masuda. A charming couple, they went out of their way to make me feel at home. They said they usually spent the summer in Canada, returning to Pakistan for the winter months. In a short time, they would be leaving again.

It was a joy to take a hot shower and tuck into a decent breakfast. Despite still feeling jaded, I accepted their invitation to tour the city, visit the Faisal Mosque, and then drive to a mountain lookout above the city. That night, I enjoyed my best sleep in a while. Reluctantly, I bade goodbye to Enum and her family before heading back to Lahore on the Daewoo Express. I was keen to get back on the bike and vowed this would be my last bus journey. As uncomfortable as the FN could be, I was at the controls, and that in itself, afforded some reassurance.

Hotel view Hunza - Pakistan

House in Hunza - Pakistan

13

What was I Thinking?

Back at Omar's, I lunched with the family, spent hours uploading photos for the blog, then went off in search of a laundry. Everything, including my grubby sleeping bag, was in need of a good cleansing.

Next day, I joined biker club members at the Pakwheels Auto Show 2012. The novelty of answering a barrage of questions about me, and the FN, soon wore off, so, at the first opportunity, I snuck away, leaving Ali & Akbar to do a splendid job of entertaining the crowd. My bike was centre stage, and the media loved it.

I wandered around admiring vintage cars, including a '60s Ford Anglia, a couple of classic motorbikes, several late-model Mercedes-Benzes and Audis, and a Ferrari. Plenty of boys have very expensive toys in Lahore.

Tahir, a visitor to the show, invited me to dinner with his family the next night, where I would meet his Kiwi friends. Hearing familiar accents was like eating 'fush-and-chups', or a meat pie — it felt comfortable. Socialising over, it was time to focus on more important things.

I'd marked out the spokes Omar had purchased for the FN, and Ali & Akbar were to have these cut and threaded while I was away. On my return, I was dismayed to find the spokes still far too long, and not threaded.

The reason was simple. After I left for the KKH, both guys checked the FN's spokes for length and decided I must have made an error. The problem was they were measuring the spokes against the front wheel, whereas the new ones were for the rear.

Rather than hang around for another day, I decided to carry the unthreaded spokes with me, in the hope of finding someone who could do the job. Omar agreed to buy additional spokes and give them to Lynne to take with her to Tehran. She would be stopping in Lahore to collect her Iranian visa, in the same way I had done.

My plan was to leave Lahore by 6.30 next morning, but TV crews wanting to film my departure kept me until nearly eight o'clock. Members of the bikers club rode with me for about an hour, when we pulled into a fuel station and said our goodbyes. I'd made many wonderful friends and was deeply indebted to them. Now, on my own again, I stopped briefly to change the carburettor jet to a smaller size. When this failed to provide the increased power I was seeking, I changed it back.

At about 3.00 pm, after 150 kilometres, I pulled into a truck stop, more generally known in Pakistan as a truck hotel. I knew that by the time I had washed, eaten and recounted my story a dozen times, I'd be ready for bed. All day long people had yelled and waved as I passed, many stopping me just to say, 'I saw you on television'.

Whenever I parked a crowd gathered, most wanting photographs taken with the bike. With everyone wielding a mobile phone, it was an odd sensation to know my picture was being beamed hither and yon, possibly to every corner of the world.

Truck hotels in Pakistan are more elaborate and tidier than their Indian equivalents. Often there are tables and chairs outdoors, and they have central cooking areas. The driveway approaches are in better condition, because vehicles tend to be parked on the roadside rather than driven in. Driving standards also seem better than in India, but it may be that my mind is playing tricks.

Overnight, the truck hotel's generator broke down, and although fixing it meant another late departure for me, I was happy to oblige. Fortunately, all the FN needed was an adjustment to the front wheel bearings. My destination that day was Multan, 247 kilometres away.

By lunch I was just over halfway and making good time. I stopped at a roadside restaurant and downed three bowls of kibria, a delicious steamy Chinese-style soup, before setting off again. I was carrying a photo of Nazir, a man I'd met in Hay, N.S.W. He was back in Australia studying for four years, and I wanted to give his wife and family in Multan a photo I'd taken of him posing with the FN. But it wasn't to be. For hours I searched for the address Nasir had given me. Finally I gave up, and asked at a fuel stop if I could camp there for the night. Riaz, who worked there, offered me a place to kip at his house. We locked the FN inside the building, and I accepted a ride on his bike, to a small shed he rented. 'You can sleep here, Uncle,' he offered, pointing to the only bed in the room. I politely declined, and bedded down on a pile of corncobs, with just a dusty sack for cover.

Bone-weary, hungry and covered in mosquito bites, I back was on the road at dawn, when Riaz started his next shift. I managed only a few kilometres before the remaining few unbroken spokes on the right-hand side of the rear wheel collapsed. Things looked grim, until I tracked down a bicycle repairer who offered to fix them. I wasn't sure he could, but, with no alternative, I agreed he should try. I removed the wheel, stripped it and handed over a bundle of new, blank spokes that needed shortening, and rethreading. To my horror, the repairer cut off the bent ends that go through the hub! Agape, I watched as he shortened the spokes and bent new hooks, successfully retaining the original threading on the other end. I breathed a sigh of relief. The man was a genius!

That seemingly happy ending to a bad start to the day had me feeling my luck was in. Wrong! The perversity of well-intentioned human kindness was about to give me a bad time.

I happened to be in the market area of the village, and eight or so policemen were hanging around, some pretending to control the traffic or the crowd, others just exposing their self-importance.

The senior police officer 'helpfully' ordered the local tyre specialist to fit and inflate the tyre on the repaired wheel. Aware that no one around had experience with beaded-edge tyres, I tried to object, but the police chief stopped me short.

'You'll insult the man if you don't let him do the job,' he ordered, handing me a bottle of cola and insisting I take a seat. Fidgety, I still tried to instruct the tyre man — and still the cop urged me to let him alone. My hackles were rising. Just as I expected, as soon as he began inflating the tube, the tyre came off the rim and the tube exploded. And so did I.

'Relax, he'll fix it,' the policeman urged, patting me on the shoulder. I shook him off. Teeth clenched, I unpacked another tube from the pannier. Before I could grab the wheel from the tyre specialist, two policemen pushed me back.

'It will be alright. He is an expert, ' they insisted. I ran my hands through my hair, sighing audibly.

Sure, it was the man's compressor and his tools that were being used, but it was a tricky job — and I knew how to do it! I tried even more vehemently to explain the correct procedure, but either the guy couldn't understand or he was determined to do it his own way.

Bang! It happened again. Lost for words, I stared at my hands as if they held the answer. The man said something to the officer I couldn't quite hear.

'What did he say?' I asked, my voice surprisingly measured.

'He said the tube is faulty.'

'Bullshit, they were perfectly new tubes.'

'No,' he insisted, 'The first time was a mistake. But this one was perished. Look at the hole.'

His lips curling in a Mona Lisa smile.

I couldn't believe I was hearing this, and snorted loudly: 'He's managed to ruin two new tubes. So much for being an expert!'

The crowd moved in closer, sensing a showdown. And I was losing face by showing anger: the cop was top of the heap, and I was undermining his authority. I had only one tube left and couldn't afford to risk handing it over. Yet I did — for the third fucking time! And, for the third time, the new tube burst.

I honestly don't know what made me risk that last precious tube. I carried a spark-plug pump, which had done the inflation job adequately in the past, but for some reason I wasn't thinking rationally and forgot about it. The combination of crowd and strong police presence had rattled me. Under pressure to have the job done quickly, I had foolishly capitulated. Whatever was I thinking? My cheeks flamed. I wanted to flee. But I no longer had any tubes, and I didn't have a clue where, this late in the day, I could find new ones.

The police were in the village in force because a politician was due to arrive any minute. 'You can get them in the next town,' said one policeman, matter-of-factly. His senior officer wanted me to move on before the dignitary arrived. For once, I had to agree with him: no one wants the village idiot hanging around. A pick-up truck driver was ordered to load the bike and take it to a workshop, back in Multan — where, of course, I found no 21-inch tubes.

I was furious at myself for not insisting on being left alone to do the job; and frustrated that the need for 'respect' took precedence over common sense.

Hell, I'm surprised I didn't take the tube out of the front wheel and hand that to him as well!

Now, not only did I have no way of continuing, I also had no accommodation for the night. As luck would have it, just when I'd thought I'd be sleeping in a ditch for the night, Lynne called from Australia, and within minutes she'd found a hotel close by and booked a room. I gave a big thank-you to modern technology, and to my clear-thinking partner.

My plan from there was to ride west on N70 to Quetta, 586 kilometres away. That proved impossible, the manager telling me the road was open only to the military and locals. Outsiders found on this route, he said, were being sent back to Multan. So my only option was to take N5 south to Sukkur, then head north on N65 to Quetta. This would add 272 kilometres to my journey.

When I called Ali from Multan that night he agreed to go to the market to get replacement tubes and courier them to the Hotel Sindbad, where I was staying. I felt guilty as Ali & Akbar — who had already done so much for me — were about to leave on a motorcycling tour, and my request had set their departure back a day. Almost weepy, I gratefully thanked my friend, and settled in for the wait.

Overloaded at truck hotel - Pakistan

14

Effie

Thankfully, after the usual daily power cut had ended and the hotel's hot water system began working, I could take a shower. It made all the difference: not just in being clean, but it restored my energy, putting me in a calmer frame of mind. Although the bed looked enticing I was hanging out for a good meal and went in search of something familiar. The restaurant's one page menu didn't include much I recognised, except for milkshakes. Well at least that's what it said.

'What flavours do you have?' I asked.

'Sorry Sir, no milkshakes.'

'But it says milkshakes.'

'Yes, but no milkshakes.'

'What about the iced coffee?'

'No iced coffee.'

'Why?'

'Well Sir, we make an ordinary coffee then it takes fifteen minutes to make it cold, and then we have to add the ice cream,' he replied.

I sighed. 'Well, do you have chips?'

'Yes Sir, we have chips.'

So a big plate of chips it was. They wouldn't get the Heart Foundation's tick of approval, but sod it. I needed some comfort food.

That night I reflected on why so often I seemed to repeat the same mistakes. It was frustrating having to struggle to be understood, and even harder to be patient when everything went wrong. Being 'stranded' in a crowd, when all I wanted to do was crawl in a corner and sit in silence to think clearly, proved to be the most exasperating of all my challenges. It was the loss of control that was hardest to handle and yet I had to question if at any time I was ever in control?

On the days when all was going well I thought I had a handle on it. If my old motorcycle was bopping along nicely I felt I could achieve anything. But then we'd hit a pothole, break a few spokes and everything changed. In retrospect, there were many things I could have done differently to avoid this day turning to crap. I didn't need to spend hours chuffing needlessly around Multan looking for an address. Covering 250 kilometres a day was a recipe for disaster and I needed a reminder that this sort of lunacy never bodes well.

After an hour of fruitless searching I could have said, 'Stuff it' and ticked that one off my list. But, I wanted to give a photo of Nasir posing with the FN to his new wife and family, who no doubt all missed him terribly. But it wasn't to be.

Next day, true to their word, Ali and Akbar got the new tubes to me. I returned to the workshop where the bike was stored. Fitting the tube and tyre proved so easy when I was left to my own devices.

I needed to get a shim made to adjust the crown wheel. It had to be 0.7mm thick. Had I been able to make it understood that all I needed was a piece of tin and a pair of tin snips, I could have cut out one in 15 minutes. But no: the workshop men, after being gone for four hours, returned, proudly showing me a shim they'd had manufactured. It was 1.5mm thick!

Why did I keep doing this? I couldn't seem to help myself. People always did their best to be helpful, usually professing to know far more than they did. It was as if that, by saying they couldn't do something, they would lose face. Even if they had experience working on modern motorcycles, coping with a veteran machine needed all sorts of other knowledge and skills. By not wanting to be condescending or unappreciative, I kept allowing myself to be sucked in every time.

I sighed, and set about doing what I should have done in the first place: rummage around for something that would fit the bill — among the rubbish, I found a used oilcan — and, with scissors, I cut a correct-size shim in minutes.

I now had the bike assembled, but it was getting too late to leave town, and the workshop was going to be closed next day. It was twilight, and with my hotel at least three kilometres away, it didn't make sense to ride there. The editor of a local newspaper, the daily *Sadaat News*, suggested I push the bike about four doors up the road and leave it in his office overnight. When I got there, he assured me the FN would be safe. He opened his desk drawer to reveal a loaded gun. 'The nightwatchman will be here soon, and he takes care of any problems,' he said with a grin.

Truck drivers - Pakistan

Overloaded truck on way to Quetta - Pakistan

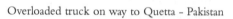

In the morning, I found my bike still in safe hands. In appreciation, before leaving for Bhawalpur, I gave the editor an interview for his newspaper.

My heart was in my mouth from the start of that leg. The rear wheel was no longer running true, so more broken spokes seemed inevitable. Fortunately, this didn't happen that day, which was just as well given my phone could reach no one.

The chilly 6.00 am start soon gave way to a sunny cloudless sky. My ride across dry, barren plains was going to be a warm one. Like mine tailings, the sand was piled high alongside the road. By the time I reached Ahmedpur, to the south, I'd removed my thermals and jacket; and after lunch I searched for a quiet place to rest. A shopkeeper suggested I take a nap in the mosque. I was just about to do his bidding, when he returned. 'Please, you must move. It is too dangerous to leave the bike unguarded.' So I sat by the FN. The man was still worried, but I was tired and reluctant to move again. He went away, and returned a few moments later with a piece of cardboard. I should lie on it, he said. I rested until mid-afternoon, then, rode on for a few more hours.

The power in the bike was now so low I doubted it would get far next day. That evening, at a truck hotel, I replaced the rings in the number-one cylinder and took advantage of the hotel's heavy cutters to chop and bend several new spokes. I'd bought a map of the area but it was useless. When I spoke with Lynne later, she familiarised me with the local geography.

Pakistan, like India, is full of colourful characters. One wizened old man in a red-and-green tunic sported, on the front of his bicycle, matching coloured flags and a large photo of the late Benazir Bhutto. Well before sunrise, when I broke camp to head for Sukkur, he was also setting out for the day, ready to extol Bhutto's virtues to all and sundry.

Wrecks litter the roads through Pakistan, and I saw many vehicles in which it was obvious the occupants had not survived. The farther I travelled, the less I thought of Pakistani driving skills.

Motoring on across seemingly endless flat wasteland, here and there I passed clusters of drab mud houses. Vegetation was sparse, only tussock grass surviving the heat of a relentless sun. After again seeking shelter in a truck hotel, I returned from photographing an old stone arched bridge to be greeted by university students who invited me to share their dinner of vegetable pancakes and yoghurt in their rather cramped campus quarters across the road.

I enjoyed the conversation, which made me realise that at times my travels, as well as gruelling, were proving very lonely.

Onlookers - Pakistan

Fitting new spokes - Pakistan

Truck hotel kitchen on the road to Quetta - Pakistan

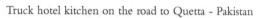

More and more, I found myself talking to the motorcycle, so much so, that I felt she deserved a name. So it was Effie.

I'd been mostly happy with Effie's power since changing the rings, and all still appeared to be going well apart from a repetitive 'clicky-clacking' noise, which now seemed more pronounced. Maybe I was imagining it, or simply the sun was frying my brain. Effie and I chattered away for miles, coaxing each other to go just a little further before the next rest stop. I sang to her, mainly songs from the 1960s. I didn't know any from 1910.

Because of the heat, I only managed 26 kilometres that morning before pulling into a café. The Coca-Cola was cold and quenching. I asked a policeman why all the trucks were overloaded. Knowingly, he replied: 'Because then they only have to do one journey. It would take two trucks to carry the legal load.'

Logical, my dear officer, logical!

By lunch, I had travelled 60 kilometres. After a rest in the shade, I battled on. In eight hours of riding, I covered a mere 140 kilometres. Passersby still waved or stopped me, but fewer mentioned seeing me on television. Already I was yesterday's news. It was still 250 kilometres to Quetta, which would be a significant milestone. I was aware the region was tightly controlled.

As I rested on the wide, mud-brick windowsill of the truck hotel, the moon full and a desert breeze on my face, I thought back to a time when I slept on a sled in Alaska and gazed, awestruck, at the magical green-and-red patterns of an aurora borealis weaving in the sky. And I got to thinking also of all those students with whom I had shared that stuffy, mosquito-ridden dormitory. In Pakistan, students are unlikely to have much time for mooning over heavenly wonders; for them, the imperative is to get a good education.

Just as I was nodding off, the local constabulary arrived, insisting that I follow them to the nearby police station. 'What's the problem, everything seems okay,' I offered. 'You're a tourist, and it is not safe after dark. You must come with us.'

I was hoping I could have been on my own for another day or two, but they appeared genuinely concerned for my safety, which was understandable given our proximity to the Afghan border. I knew that, from Quetta onwards, the police would play a role in my progress. They were just doing their job. Asserting my independence might have put me offside with the law — and that made no sense — so, reluctantly, I packed my gear. In no time at all, Effie and I were locked up in a police cell for the night.

Top of Bolan Pass - Pakistan

View from top of Bolan Pass - Pakistan

15

Beyond the Limits

It was April 5, two months to the day since I left Australia. With many rest stops along the way, I had ridden 182 kilometres since leaving the police post at Sibi. Quetta was still 68 kilometres ahead. Once again, I was out of phone and internet range — and aware that Lynne would be anxious.

We'd talked about the risks of travelling through dangerous regions, but she had always backed my route plans and never complained about me putting my life in danger, thereby causing others to worry. Still, I knew she would be concerned until I got back in touch.

Effie had broken another five spokes in the rear wheel, all originals, but the replacement modified spokes were doing a good job. All that they needed, as they were settling in, was retensioning each night. The front wheel, thankfully, was running true after my problem with the collapsed bearings. The past few days of slogging over broken roads had been torturous. I was hoping conditions would improve. They didn't. They got worse.

The road to Quetta was the worst I had experienced. Road reconstruction work was going on for miles. The deep holes and rough surface made steering the little bike almost impossible. At times Effie was jarred so violently I expected to hear the sound of breaking metal. Sometimes thoughts about giving in snuck up on me. But that didn't make sense because I would still have to get myself out of that hellhole. So I pressed on. All day Effie lurched from one pothole to the next. Every bone in my body ached. I can only imagine what Effie was feeling.

Sometimes I got the impression that people were telling me that the road was about to get better. However, given I couldn't speak Urdu, they might as well have been telling me Iran was just around the bend. Sixty kilometres seemed like 600 as I battled over broken asphalt.

In some places, vehicles found it easier going to get off the road and travel on the sand alongside it. This wasn't an option for me: century-old bikes don't go well off-road. Frequently, where the road surface had crumbled badly, I had to get off and push — to try to ride over those stretches could have caused serious damage to the frame.

My eyes felt as though they were being pricked by needles, my throat burned, and every breath became more laboured than the one before. The combination of heat exhaustion and lousy road conditions was threatening to push me over the edge. I was battling through the longest day of my life.

I had visions of a clean hotel, a cool shower and soft bed, but they would not be a reality that night. Instead, I slept in another very basic truck hotel. Then I got to wondering: how does anyone survive in that part of the world, where all that life promises is a harsh struggle, day in and day out? It shows in the faces of people: many, I am sure, appear much older than their years. It is as if the desert has scoured their features. Truck drivers do it especially hard. They live in dust and grime most of the time, and chai and biscuits seem to be their main sustenance. Life on the road offers them no respite until they reach the occasional stop.

For the past week, I'd been using purifying tablets, courtesy of my Australian friend Wally. They eased my doubts about the quality of what I was drinking. Having managed to avoid getting really sick so far, I still kept my fingers crossed.

Lack of contact with the outside world was gnawing at my already jaded nerves. With phone connection intermittent, I had no luck reaching Lynne, even for a few moments.

As we neared Quetta, the frequency of security checks intensified. Wanting to avoid the police, I snuck into a truck hotel, unseen. There, the management hid Effie in a place where I could work on the broken spokes before hitting the sack.

Omar had advised me not to try to go over the Bolan Pass, saying it was likely to be too steep for Effie to tackle. But next day, bored with endlessly flat desert, I decided to see if she was up to the challenge.

Two things changed dramatically: the desert became hilly and the hot dry winds gave way to strong, colder winds that were near freezing by the time I reached the summit at 1,850 metres. Drab, flat-roofed mudbrick houses blended into the hillsides.

Frequent stops were necessary to allow the engine to cool. On one of them, I chatted with friendly shopkeepers. Well, that was stretching things a bit: I said 'Australia' a few times, unaware of whether I was understood or not; and I didn't understand a word of what was said to me. I found it incongruous that we were so close to a war zone, yet life seemed so normal.

Overnight, on the Bolan Pass, I camped on the roadside, even though the road was very narrow with few places to pull off. Throughout the night, trucks were constantly wending their way up and down the steep slopes. It was dangerous to be so close to the traffic, but there were no options as it was too dark to push on. But, come the dawn, the scenery that greeted me was breathtaking. It was well worth the effort it took to get there.

As I hit the road again, my eyes widened to the wonders that lay before me. Momentarily, I forgot everything; there was not a care in me! I'd travelled through many countries down the years, and seen much magnificent scenery, most of it green and lush. This was different: the starkness of rolling ochre hills, and the wide dry riverbeds took my breath away. I'd never imagined a scene like this.

At a checkpoint near Quetta, the circus that is sub-continental bureaucracy swept back into full swing — but now the process was different. Previously, when I handed over my passport, it was inspected by every official present, before the book entries were signed, and I was sent on my way.

This time, I was given a police escort for a kilometre. Then an army escort took over. Finally, the army handed me back to a police escort, which took me all the way to the entrance of the Hotel Bloomstar, where I was told I had to stay. All up, the escort time consumed four hours, and we had travelled a distance of 62 kilometres.

At one point, I had to cross the road to a police post and then cross back, my new escort in tow. All of us risked life and limb as we moved between speeding trucks, buses and carts.

Bloody hell, if this went on, it would be spring 2015 before I even reached Europe! I hoped that this wasn't going to become the norm — having to do three push starts in succession within such a short time was no fun.

Next day, came a bit of luxury: a breakfast of toast, jam, butter and coffee. And, in a further concession from the Bloomstar management, I was allowed to park Effie on the verandah outside my room rather than in the hotel's car park. I took the opportunity to remove the barrels and check the big ends. Everything appeared fine. Had I been imagining that 'clicky-clacking'?

I had woken during the night with a sore gut. I knew there was a doctor in the next room, but rather than disturb him, I figured a couple of Gastro Stop pills would do the job. The doctor, in Quetta for a medical convention, next day kindly translated my travel plan into Urdu. I was hoping that this piece of paper would help me when I was next enduring an inevitable barrage of questions.

It was in Quetta that I learned that three days previously there had been trouble in Gilgit. Sixteen people had died and more than 50 were injured. It seems a grenade thrown into the crowd had started the violence, after which armed men herded passengers off buses and shot them before setting the vehicles on fire.

I found it hard to get my head around this news. I had been in Gilgit just two weeks before, travelling for agonisingly long hours on those same dilapidated buses, at times, waiting like a sitting duck for the landslides to be cleared. My heart went out to all those caught up in the violence, and I hoped the people who had been so kind and generous to me had not been affected.

Try as I might, I couldn't shake the images from my mind: buses crowded with women returning from market, bearded men wrapped in brown shawls to ward off the cold, and babes-in-arms who'd peered at me with huge, dark, almond eyes. I shuddered, recalling how I'd brushed off the police escorts' warning that the area was dangerous. Yes, it was, I realised that now and I had been lucky. But, was it worse than when a madman went on a killing spree in Tasmania some years before, killing 35 innocent people and injuring 23? It seems that, no matter where one is in the world, murderous violence can strike at any time.

16

Under Escort

Quetta? Streets with fetid water in open sewers; taxis jostling with battered, overloaded buses; handcarts thrusting to and fro among frenzied traffic; men in shalwar kameez selling brightly coloured shrubs and flowers; and, because it is near the Afghan border, a frequent target for terrorist bombers. I was feeling decidedly uneasy.

The owner of an internet café made me a cup of tea and helped me send photos and emails. His computers were aged and bulky, but they did the job, and his kindness was appreciated. I was only in Quetta for two nights, so it was probably my last chance to catch up with laundry and general bike maintenance before crossing into Iran.

By chance, I met Hayashi, a 25-year-old Japanese motorcyclist travelling on a tiny 110cc Honda from Malaysia to Europe. He was just leaving the hotel when we met in the foyer. His intention was to put his bike on a bus that was going across the border. He didn't get far because the driver refused to take responsibility for a foreigner. So Hayashi came back to the Bloomstar. Dejected, he asked if he could accompany me to Iran. 'Sure,' I said. 'I'd be glad of some company other than the police, especially as, from here on, things are about to get challenging.'

A group of young men, some of whom I'd met previously, stopped by the hotel for afternoon tea and a chat. My need, however, was for a really wholesome meal, but I was in for another disappointment. It seems the cook was Christian, and, because it was Easter, no meals were being prepared. This surprised me, Pakistan being a predominantly Muslim country.

I left the hotel in search of other options, but soon gave up. I just couldn't bring myself to cross those open drains to get into a restaurant. I settled for chocolates and wrapped snacks. My resolve to eat sensibly most of the time was proving difficult to maintain.

Back at the Bloomstar, the manager had a gift for me. 'Here is something to take to help you remember Pakistan,' he said, shyly, handing me a felt topi, traditional Pakistani headwear. On me, the hat looked comical, but what a lovely gesture!

A police escort of two armed guards arrived in a pick-up at 7.00 next morning — 30 minutes before we planned to leave. Immediately they began hassling us to get going. By the time we'd covered 18 kilometres, we'd had six escorts, each one taking us a short distance before handing over to another couple of guards. We sensed this was going to be a painfully slow journey, despite the increased speed we were forced to travel at. The escorts were mandatory: it is the only way foreigners are permitted to travel through this highly sensitive region of Pakistan.

When Effie experienced a loss of power, I stopped at a toll plaza to adjust the magneto points. Ignoring what I was doing, the police urged Hayashi and me to join the convoy of buses and cars. I refused: it was important that I try to boost the bike's power; and, besides, there was no way Effie, in her condition, could keep up with the convoy.

As we waited for another escort, I lay on my back under the bike trying to reset the points, all the time answering the questions of curious onlookers. Hayashi, meanwhile, was getting a bit agitated, and badgering the toll attendants about when the next escort would arrive. He was eager to get on his way, so I suggested he leave on his own, telling him I'd catch up.

Off he went, but it was not long before he was back: he had met a convoy travelling in the opposite direction and been forced by its escort to come back. Another hour passed before the new escort arrived. It was hot, the traffic was noisy, and I'd long finished the magneto job.

Soon after we got moving again, the road got worse than the one on which I'd travelled on my way to Quetta. Craters scarred the surface, and some inclines were steeper even than those I'd met in Nepal. At times, I had to grab either the side of the escort van or Hayashi's bike for a tow. The switchbacks, steep and sharp, had way too much camber. They were especially dangerous downhill for a bike with little or no braking capacity.

Despite strong winds on the way to Nushki, we had managed 150 kilometres so far that day. Feeling exhausted, and with the escort ahead of us, Hayashi and I snuck into a truck stop and hid our bikes. Optimistically, we were hoping we'd given the police the slip. Not so. Soon they were back — telling us we had to move on, because it wasn't safe to spend the night there.

Hayashi - Dalbandin, Pakistan

I was knackered, my mouth parched, every bone ached and my eyes were dull. But we obviously had no choice: it was back into police care. They told us the next police post was 50 kilometres ahead, so we slogged on, this time with our guardians close behind. But I'd had enough. I stopped and staggered off the bike, wiping a grimy face on my sleeve. My knees gave out and I collapsed to the ground. That was when the young, bearded police officer pulled alongside and told us we had passed the police post by 20 kilometres.

'Why the fuck didn't you stop us,' I exploded, incredulous he hadn't told us when we were passing it. No police posts I ever saw had signs on them saying what they were.

'I thought you wanted to go to the next one,' he said, his sarcasm undisguised.

I was gobsmacked. It had been torture riding through this god-forsaken land. Surely it was apparent to him, that given the conditions we were travelling under, I wouldn't want to travel one more metre than I had to. Shaking with anger I disputed the distance he'd estimated.

'You calling me a liar?' he roared in my face. His rifle wasn't directed at me, but it was obvious he could have been pushed into using it.

Hayashi looked on meekly. For once he was saying nothing. The policeman and I glared at one another. I knew I had overstepped the mark. Some back-pedalling was needed, and I knew there was no point in making enemies in this part of the world.

But I wasn't quite ready to eat humble pie. When the escort offered to put our bikes on the back of the utility, we refused, feeling certain the machines would be given a pounding. So we stayed on our bikes, taking some satisfaction in knowing the angry cop was forced to follow us slowly back to the post we'd passed. There was still a bit of tension in the air, but the other police at the post were pleasant to us, and the evening passed without incident.

When we settled in for the night, we reckoned that we'd covered more than 200 kilometres, under awful conditions, way too far for Effie in one day. Checking the bike, I found only one spoke needed replacing. I'd been lucky. As usual, I took the precaution of packing the differential with grease.

During the night, a choking dust storm blew up, and sand, seeping through cracks of the doors, filled our ears, eyes and throats. By morning, my hair looked like a nest of steel wool. I gave it a quick rinse under the solitary tap before setting off, our target being Dalbandin, 196 kilometres away.

We knew what the first 20 kilometres was like — we'd travelled them twice already! But the ensuing seven hours, largely through deep sand-washes, were arm-wrenching. Skinny tyres inflated to 45 PSI, coupled with Effie's long wheelbase and lack of suspension, made negotiating this type of terrain painfully difficult. Even with my years of riding experience, I'm not sure how I managed to keep the FN upright in such crippling conditions.

Hayashi took a heavy fall, which wasn't surprising considering his inexperience on motorcycles. Though visibly shaken, he pulled himself together and pressed on. He told me earlier that he had crashed in Malaysia, and had shown me the large scar on the inside of his calf. His bike was overloaded, and not particularly well-balanced, but he did have the advantage of a lower seat than mine.

Despite the hard going, neither of us at any time thought of turning back. Anyway, the police wouldn't allow us to travel or camp outside their jurisdiction, so we simply had to stick with it. Food stops were our only breaks, and these were few and far between.

After we got to Dalbandin that night, and stayed at a big police post with a lock-up jail, Hayashi and I began fantasising about what we'd love to eat for dinner. Our escort agreed to take us to a restaurant. We weren't allowed to go alone, he said, because we were too close to the border. On the way, I managed to buy two 19-inch tubes as spares. I wanted 21-inch tubes, but beggars can't be choosers.

When the meal arrived, our faces fell. We'd ordered lamb shank, picturing succulent meat falling off the bone, and a mound of fresh vegetables. My plate had a large bone, and a tiny portion of meat floating in thin, colourless gravy. I took one bite and pushed the plate away. A bottle of cola to wash down the tasteless slop was the only saving grace. And the price — even after taking our escort's meal into account — was extortionate. He had chosen a different menu item, and seemed to have got a much better deal.

That night, we slept on the police post verandah in full view of the prisoners.

On April 11, on the 160 kilometres ride to Nok-kundi, I got my best fuel return so far — 26.5 kilometres to the litre. I'd been told to expect an improvement, but, with every reason to be skeptical, it was a surprise to me to find that road so well-paved.

The police at Nok-kundi, who could speak a few words of English, were much more friendly. They even allowed us to stop at a deserted house to rest in the sweltering heat. There, a man arrived wearing a waistcoat and a pawkul, a regional beret made from lamb's wool that can be rolled down for warmth. He'd walked through searing heat to ask if we'd like a cup of tea. We gratefully accepted. Off he went back to his home, soon returning with a dented aluminium teapot and five glasses. When I tried to pay him, he waved my hand away and smiled. All I could do was say, *Shukran* (thanks).

The sealed road didn't last. Soon it was back to broken asphalt and gaping holes. Thankfully, it was only 70 kilometres to Keeyi-dailil, then a further 60 to the border at Taftan. Traffic was sparse, just a few stylish Renault and Iveco semi-trailers coming from Iran. These contrasted markedly with the battered Pakistani-owned pick-ups that plied the border, carrying smuggled petrol crudely hidden under foliage.

Our luck seemed to be improving. I'd broken only one more spoke; and, for a change, we could wash ourselves. Water, which is brought to the border regions once a month by train, is usually pretty scarce.

That night, Hayashi and I spread our sleeping bags on old steel doors outside the back of the Keeyi-dailil police compound. Lying on our backs, we gazed at the heavens. We stopped counting satellites at 16. That was a real treat for Hayashi, who had never seen a satellite glide across the sky before.

When the temperature started to drop sharply, we moved inside the unfinished police building. No doors or windows had been fitted in the brick structure, so it was pretty chilly. Yet, so fatigued were we, sleep quickly overcame us.

17

Playing the Game

Greatly relieved, on April 12 we rolled into Taftan, a foul border town, no less grubby than I expected. My petrol was low, but a search revealed no official fuel outlets. Smuggled petrol, which had been emptied from 44-gallon drums into plastic jerry-cans, was selling at exorbitant prices. Usually, it was poured into vehicle tanks through sand-encrusted funnels. I carried my own funnel in the hope of avoiding contamination.

When we rode up to the customs post and waited for our carnets to be stamped, a kindly official served us super-sweet tea in small terracotta bowls, and ginger-nut biscuits. The paperwork took about 20 minutes, and then, triumphantly, Hayashi and I rode into Iran.

We beamed at each other, tired, but elated. In the previous 17 days since leave Lahore, Effie and I had had everything thrown at us — brutal roads, blinding sand storms, pushy escorts, lack of decent food, mechanical crises... too many too mention. My body had been pummeled, squeezed through a mincer, (at least that's what it felt like), and I had the scars to prove it.

In my younger, crazier days, I had completed a 24-hour endurance ride and my thoughts then, like now, were not my own — I was merely a zombie stumbling through the motions. More than once I wanted to call it quits, to load the bike on a passing truck and forget the insanity of such a journey.

But, I'd survived, despite the frustration and fatigue, and was feeling a deep sense of release to now have it all behind me. Few westerners choose to ride across Pakistan, and those who do are usually on more modern motorcycles, better equipped, and often travel in groups. I thanked Effie profusely for standing up so heroically to her task.

Despite what I had endured, I was humbled by the generosity and

Local colour – Pakistan

Police escorts – Dalbandin, Pakistan

Paperwork, Taftan border – Pakistan

kindness of the Pakistanis I had met. I had a store of wonderful memories — including of friends I had made along the way — that would remain with me forever.

I had achieved a major goal in reaching Iran. Although it is usually described as a totalitarian state by most Western governments, I'd read many favourable reports from travellers, and I was dying to get a firsthand view of the place. Nevertheless, it was with some trepidation that I entered the Iranian customs building.

I was pleasantly surprised. There were clean, modern, refrigerated food cabinets — and carton milk was available! The toilets were spotless, the place was air-conditioned, and the officials were polite and helpful.

I met a rider heading the other way, the first European long-distance motorcyclist I'd seen since leaving Nepal. We exchanged a few words, and then he headed into Pakistan. I smiled to myself, wondering if he had even the slightest idea of what lay in store.

In three hours, we were through. The officials, who insisted we would be escorted all the way to Bam, 429 kilometres to the west, wanted to ride on the back of Hayashi's bike (strangely, nobody wanted to ride my motorcycle!). When he emphatically refused, they commandeered a passing vehicle, much to its owner's dismay.

Just two kilometres further on, the police stopped us. They had been told that Hayashi's paperwork wasn't in order: he had fitted a bogus Pakistani plate to his bike and the number didn't correspond with what was written on his carnet. While he was in their office providing his explanation, I replaced the Pakistani plate with his Japanese plate. As well as sporting a beard and wearing a drab shalwar kameez, Hayashi put the false plate on in Pakistan to avoid drawing attention to himself, and he'd forgotten to swap it over before crossing the border.

Jalil, a young custom officer, presented me with cold cans of peach nectar and insisted we give him a call when we reached Zahedan, capital of Sistan and Baluchestan Province, where he lived. Before we left, he said: 'Your escort is very worried because the police have explained to him, in English, that you are both tourists. But he has interpreted that as terrorists, and does not want to take you.' We all laughed.

Once Hayashi had sorted out his paperwork, we rode on, with a police motorcycle escort in tow. We travelled about four kilometres, and then waited 45 minutes for another escort. This time, none of the escorts had vehicles of their own, so police commandeered a pick-up from a reluctant passerby, relieved us of our passports and accompanied us halfway towards Zahedan.

The delays were becoming annoying, and even more so when military escorts put our passports in their pockets and drove off. Feeling more vulnerable than ever, we decided we had to make a stand. Enough was enough, we insisted, asserting that we wouldn't continue riding this way.

The escort responded by saying that, because we were travelling too slowly, we had to load Effie and the Honda on yet another commandeered truck. My suspicion that this wasn't going to be a gentle ride was soon confirmed.

The bikes were tied on with insufficient rope to hold them securely. I planted my feet firmly and braced myself between the two bikes in an effort to prevent them hitting each other. It wasn't easy: we were traveling at 100 kmh and the bikes were swaying dangerously from side to side. I clenched my jaw and hung on tight.

By the time the vehicle finally screeched to a halt outside the Zahedan police post, my hands were clammy, my breathing rapid, and my bladder near to bursting. We waited 15 minutes and then were driven on 200 metres to another police post, this one opposite our hotel. Hayashi and I clambered down from the truck, exhausted and shaking, barely able to unload our machines.

Despite our scruffy appearance, we were made to feel welcome by friendly hotel staff. The accommodation was immaculate and modern. At $60 a night, it was way over our budget, but, because the police had ordered us to stay there, we had no choice. After yet another paper shuffle, we were free to go to our room. For the next 48 hours, we enjoyed comfortable beds, hot showers, clean clothes and — best of all — privacy.

Hayashi and I were soon tucking into a scrumptious meal. Choices of food and drink had been rare, especially since Quetta, so we relished the hotel's expansive menu. Funnily enough, despite the selection, I chose chicken-and-rice.

Next day, Hayashi and I wandered the dusty streets for hours in search of oil and petrol, and for somewhere to put air in our tyres. It was our luck to find most businesses were closed for prayers. Before we were to meet Jalil, our border-post acquaintance, I managed to buy dates, long-nosed pliers and chocolates at the markets.

Unlike most countries, it was difficult to know where, and how, to buy petrol in Iran. When I did find it, I made sure to top up my two spare 5 litre cans. I knew the tank held enough fuel for 120 kilometres and the spare fuel would see me through longer stretches.

Fuel is sold on a quota system in Iran. When I was there, Iranians were allowed $35 worth a month, and they were given a fuel card that enabled them to buy a specific number of litres at a discount price.

Initially, I found this confusing. When I saw people using fuel cards, I got the impression that they were prepaid, so I asked at service stations if I could buy one. No one seemed to know what I was talking about. I then found that, if a pump was manned, I could buy fuel with cash; otherwise, I had to rely on the generosity of locals offering their fuel cards to help me out. Some even went so far as refusing payment.

Oil, too, was not easy to find, there being no signs indicating where it was available. Rogan, as oil is known, was sold in shops, rather than fuel stations, and is usually among general goods. At one stage, I was reduced to using the miniscule amount of oil that I carried in the two tiny cans on my tank bags. Eventually, I cottoned on: where there were 44-gallon drums outside a shop, there usually was oil for sale.

Jalil gave us a tour of the city, including a visit to a museum featuring artefacts dating back to 3,000 years BC, then took us to his apartment, serving us tea, biscuits and fresh nuts.

Our friend then dropped us at an internet café, returning later to take us back to our hotel. He kindly filled the petrol can I'd been carrying and refused to accept payment. Such hospitality from someone who, a few days before had been a total stranger was most impressive, and much appreciated. Jalil's ease with English had made for a relaxing and pleasant few hours.

Next day, Hayashi and I decided that we should go our separate ways, his bike being so much faster than mine. Also, it was frustrating having to wait for escorts, who seemed to waste so much time poring over our papers. Forcing us to travel at their pace was especially hard on Effie and neither of us were happy being told what we could and couldn't do. If I'd wanted a guide, I'd have taken a bus tour! We felt that being out of Pakistan and away from known trouble spots, we didn't need company on the road. Well, it wasn't to be, even though we tried, by deception, to activate our plan. We collected our passports from the hotel desk, telling the receptionist we needed to go to the bank for money. Then, once outside, we did a runner.

Our scheme was to get to Bam. We'd figured out the route from Zahedan on our city walk the day before, so we both headed west. Just one catch: it seems the hotel staff must have called the police, because we'd only ridden about three kilometres when we heard the sirens.

Several police vehicles descended on us, the occupants directing us to the side of the road. Their aggressive attitude and shouting would have been comical if they hadn't carried pistols. The police clearly weren't impressed by what we were trying to do and each in his way tried to intimidate us. The questions came thick and fast: 'Where are you going? Why didn't you wait at the hotel? Don't you realise this place is not safe for foreigners and that you need us to escort you?'

Like guilty schoolboys, we just stood there and fidgeted. To push home their point, they spent ages scrutinising each page of our passports, before putting them in their pockets and patting them, as if to demonstrate their authority.

This time it was Hayashi who got upset. He shoved one of the policemen, and yelled, 'We know where we're heading, just let us go.' Four or five others closed around us, and a scuffle broke out between Hayashi and the officers. Things weren't looking good.

'Calm down mate, calm down,' I found myself saying. Getting ourselves thrown in a lock-up wouldn't achieve anything; they might even decide to throw away the key! Obviously, an escort was going to be mandatory, at least for a few more days.

Finally, tempers cooling, we were chaperoned out of Zahedan. One car sat immediately in front of our bikes, another close behind. For the first few hours, the escort changed every 30 kilometres or so, then we went much longer distances before there was a change of bodyguards. All the time, we were being urged to speed up. I understood the sense of urgency in getting us through the restricted zone as quickly as possible, but this just wouldn't work for Effie — it was ridiculous to expect her to maintain such an insane pace.

My preferred routine was to stop regularly, rest the motor and check the bike. Because of the forced high pace, I was pumping more oil into the engine than I knew was needed because there was no way of guessing when the level was correct. I knew that if I saw oil dripping onto my boot everything was well lubricated. And I was afraid to push Effie any harder.

As if this wasn't enough to contend with, there was another surprise in store. Suddenly, searing winds hit, blasting sand across the road, the grains cutting into our faces. We had covered 235 kilometres, but now visibility was down to a few metres.

Many times I came close to falling as I strained to keep the bike upright in the violent cross-wind. My arms felt as if they were being torn from their sockets. It was when we pulled into the police post to swap escorts — and we had only five litres of spare fuel between us — Hayashi and I insisted we could go no further.

It had been a bloody long haul, and we knew there was no chance of making it to Bam before nightfall. So we were stuck with another tough night in a police post. I got off the bike and, leaning into the wind, stumbled into the room. Hayashi and I sagged to floor, totally spent.

The post was a simple affair, and what little water there was had been trucked in. The only toilet had a grubby bowl, and there were no sleeping quarters.

I suspect the police knew we'd noticed where they had stored our passports, because a while later they ushered us into another room, where we bedded down on the floor. At least this time we were given extra blankets.

Quickly, we fell into sleep, only to be just as quickly woken and given a meal of chicken-and-rice. It was very welcome, especially as all we'd had between us that day was a handful of raisins. For someone who hates rice, I seemed to have been eating a hell of a lot of it in recent weeks — but I wasn't complaining.

Before I closed my eyes, and succumbed to the dreams of the demented, I chuckled to myself, thinking how ludicrous it was to imagine that I could have eluded the police on a century-year-old motorcycle; or to think Hayashi and I had even contemplated grabbing our passports from the drawer and making another dash for it. We definitely needed our heads read!

Our desert shelter near Kerman - Iran

Bam Citadel - Iran

18

Desert Rendezvous

Under a clear sky, we prepared to travel the few remaining kilometres to Bam. Effie had other ideas: she had no compression. I removed the spark plugs, added a few drops of oil to the pistons, and put the plugs back — and she started. Well, sort of. We were able to move off, but she would not rev. So I dismantled the carburettor. It was full of sand from the horrors of the previous day. Using a little of my precious fuel, I washed it out sparingly. Problem solved.

We drove on to Bam and found Akbar's Guest House, a home-stay, without much trouble. That's where we were told we would from then on be allowed to travel without escort. The police handed us our passports and wished us well. This last group, much more appreciative of my speed limitations, had allowed us to travel at our own pace for the final leg.

During one of my nightly Skype sessions with Lynne, I had mentioned that I wondered why people kept refusing payment for the petrol they bought for my bike.

'What are you saying to them?' she asked.

'Nothing. I just show them the scrap of paper that Jalil translated for me into Persian. It says, 'Can you help me buy petrol?'

'Maybe it doesn't read exactly what you intended,' said Lynne.

'You could be right. I'm now wondering if they think I'm on a pilgrimage and that their donation will help me on my way.'

Only later, when someone who spoke English and read my note, did the light dawn. Basically, the message was asking everyone to buy petrol for me! I recalled one man, after he had filled my tank, said, 'We're all terrorists right?' It was embarrassing to realise that the note might have come across as if I was begging. My mistake.

Akbar's, a two-level brick building in a gated compound, was slightly damaged in the devastating earthquake of 2003, in which more than 26,000 people died and 30,000 were injured. Although reconstruction was still under way, there were kitchen facilities, hot water and a decent shower block. Even better, no longer were armed guards watching my every move.

When Hayashi said goodbye after breakfast, and set off on his own, I was once more back in control of my life. Now I could decide when I stopped to rest; how long I stayed in each place; and, more importantly, I was able to treat Effie a good deal more gently. What a difference that made! I was still amazed at her resilience considering the horrific demands I'd put on her. Even on good roads, it was a big ask for an old girl of her vintage.

Kaveh, a German traveller staying at Akbar's, accompanied me on the long walk to the reconstruction site of the ancient city of Bam which dates back 2000 years. We spent three hours wandering the narrow streets of the Arg-e Bam citadel. Scaffolding everywhere, mud bricks strewn about. Before the quake, this was the largest mud-brick construction in the world, covering an area of 180,000 square metres. Its seven metre-high mud-brick walls are right out of *The Arabian Nights*. We were able to see only about 20 per cent of the old city because many unrestored areas were still sectioned off, too unstable for the public to enter. I wondered how the people who lived there could ever recover from such tragedy.

On the way back to Akbar's, we stopped for lunch at a restaurant and I tucked into a freshly made hamburger, Iranian style. It made a nice change from chicken-and-rice.

Foreign currency was in big demand. In the banks, while $US1 was equivalent to 12,250 rials, on the black market it was possible to get 18,500. Jewellers, among other traders, as well as people on the street, would ask if I had money to exchange, so keen were they to get their hands on US currency.

At Akbar's, I met Yan and Martin, two guys from the Czech Republic, who were riding their motorcycles through Iran. I hadn't yet come across many European travellers, but I expected that would change once I reached Turkey.

My gear was clean, the bike readied, it was time to leave Bam. Mohammed, Akbar's son, had arranged to have the stitching on my panniers repaired. Despite being unwell, Mohammed was a kind and generous host. I left Akbar's carrying his gift of delicious yellow dates. They were my first real treat in weeks, and I was looking forward to sharing what I had left of them with Lynne when next we met.

Hayashi had texted to warn me to don extra warm clothes on the ride to Kerman. The weather there, he said, was freezing. It wasn't until I started to see snow on the roadside that I realised just how cold it was going to be.

The only problems I encountered in Iran until then had been the occasional crazy motorcyclist who, without indicating, darted in front of Effie. Generally, road users were kind and courteous. At one fuel station, Abrahim, the owner, made me a cup of sweet black tea and served it with bread & cheese.

He also offered me two watermelons. I know it can be considered impolite to refuse a gift, but where the heck was I going to put those huge fruit? Perhaps my note explaining what I was doing should have included, 'Sorry, I have no room for watermelons!'

Having had a blow-out in India, I'd been worried the replacement tyre wouldn't last. I needn't have, because, having already covered 3000 kilometres, it still had a third of its rubber remaining. I could get to Tehran before putting on a new one. Knowing there were spare tyres waiting for me in Tehran took a weight off my mind. The only broken spokes in recent days had been those that were on the bike when I left Australia. The spokes that I had made for me in Pakistan were proving stronger, so that was something else I didn't need to fret about.

As the desert road steadily climbed between the mountain ranges, their peaks covered in heavy snow, I realised I should have altered the carburettor jet before leaving Bam. When I stopped for lunch, with 147 kilometres behind me, I was shivering. It was time for my thermals.

I pressed on for a while, but even with extra clothing I felt I couldn't make it much farther. Just 30 kilometres short of Kerman, I spent the night in an abandoned house Hayashi had told me about. For the first time, I used my self-inflating camping mattress, wondering why the heck I'd never unrolled it before. Despite its thin profile, I enjoyed my best sleep of the journey so far.

It was early morning when I rolled into Kerman. I set about looking for the Akvahan Hotel, but, after several misdirections, and failing to find it, I checked into the Govashir Hotel. It charged 700,000 rials a night, but, for the moment, it just wasn't worth the hassle trying to save a few dollars.

My plan was to spend time exploring Kerman, and to catch up with Ali, a young guy I'd met in Bam. When we met, he showed me to the cheaper Akvahan Hotel. Then he and his girlfriend, Fatimah, drove me to the Shazdeh Gardens (Prince's Gardens) at nearby Mahan, a desert oasis. There we joined a group of their friends and wandered through the terraced gardens with stately mosaic-tiled buildings, pools and ornamental fountains.

It was then on to a teahouse, where I tried a peach-flavoured hookah. To everyone's amusement, I failed, in several attempts, to get the hang of this hubble-bubble. The hookah is popular with Iranians, but it did nothing for me. I preferred ice cream instead.

Later that day, we drove out into the desert for a picnic. By parking the two cars side by side, and stretching a blanket over them, we had some protection from a vicious wind. We huddled together, enjoying chicken, bread, salad and cola, and swapping yarns while the radio played Iranian pop music. I was moved that these young people should have time for an old bloke like me.

Back in Kerman, we admired the magnificent 750-year-old Masjid Jame Mosque, and a fascinating 2,000-year-old round stone building, origin unknown. Ali was taking pictures with a camera he'd bought new six months previously for $150. Inflation, he said, meant the same camera was now selling for $230. I hoped the world's embargo on Iran would soon be lifted.

The following day, we visited the Vakil Bazaar, reputed to be one of the oldest trading centres in Iran. On one of its portals, is a foundation inscription date of 1598.

Hayashi had texted me, 'Don't miss it'. The bazaar certainly is magnificent. Row upon row of stalls offering food, clothing, pots, brassware (you name it) and teashops are cheek-by-jowl under high-domed ceilings.

Later, as I wandered the city, I got chatting with Mohammed, whose bookshop sells many popular Western publications, including an Iranian version of Colleen McCullough's *Thornbirds*. It was Mohammed who told me where to find the R-clips I was searching for, and then hailed a taxi to take me there. The driver insisted it was necessary, by law, to use the seatbelt in the back. That made me smile: the belt was a five centimetre wide strip of black elastic that, in an event of an accident, would likely have catapulted me through the front or rear window!

I was sorry to leave Kerman. I'd been fascinated by this historic city, and all it has to offer. My friendship with Ali had made Kerman a highlight of my journey so far.

The smooth sealed highway, ribboning across the open brown desert, helped me equal my previous best fuel economy. At the Sherif Abaz truckstop, while I was tucking into a tasty lunch, a group of men joined me. One was Alireza, a long-distance truck driver, hauling goods between Paris and Kerman every two weeks. Another guy at the table invited me to his home for the night, explaining that his father was long dead and his elderly mother was lonely. There were smiles and chuckles among the group, and I got the feeling — with all the nudge-nudge, wink-winking going on — that my services would be appreciated. I politely declined, insisting I would sleep at the truckstop.

Around 8.00 pm, I prepared to bed down on a bench outside the fast-food shop. At midnight, Yasser, the owner, woke me to say that I must put the bike inside the shop and also sleep in there. He handed me the key and asked that I give it to the first person that came by in the morning, or take it to an address around the corner. He then left for home. Next morning, when nobody arrived, I woke the tyre repairman next door and gave him the key before going on my way.

It was desert as far as the eye could see for the next 197 kilometres to Yazd. Amid the arid desolation, Yazd is a green and beautiful oasis, resplendent with lush gardens and tranquil parks.

Effie did well on the run from Kerman, although the higher altitude affected her carburettor settings. When I arrived at the Hotel Kohan in Kashane, and parked her in the lobby, she was definitely in need of a service.

Needing a file, I walked into town and found a Honda shop, where the owner told his foreman to take me on his motorcycle to another shop. When I selected two files, yet again, I was dealing with someone who refused payment.

Next morning I found Effie dwarfed by an XRV 750 Baja Honda Twin belonging to Roemer and Lisan, a Dutch couple on a world tour. Together we walked into Yazd, and, over lunch, we shared experiences. We decided that, next day, we would visit the Yazd Water Museum, which tells the story of how Iran's desert peoples have found and stored water. Unfortunately, the museum was closed, so, instead, Baba Basani's ice cream parlour had to do.

Roemer and Lisan headed east to Pakistan, while I pressed on in the opposite direction towards Isfahan. I was booked to stay the night at the Tak-Taku Homestay in the small town of Toudeshk, but 80 kilometres before Nain my rear tyre burst, causing the bike to weave erratically. This had happened before, and each time I had been fortunate not to end up in the path of oncoming traffic. I was lucky again...

Seven spokes broke when that tyre burst, and it was three punishing hours before I had fixed everything and trued up the wheel. I couldn't complain: that tyre had endured more than 3,500 kilometres, and the 30-year-old tyre on the somewhat lighter front end was continuing to hold out well.

While I was working on the bike, several people stopped to offer assistance, moving on when they could see I had things under control. It was good not to be constantly surrounded by onlookers, and to be able to focus on the task in hand in peace.

By the time I was ready to ride again, the light had gone. Feeling unable to make it to Toudeshk safely in the dark, I pulled into a truck-repair shop. Pointing to a semi-trailer, I asked the shop owner, 'Can I sleep on the back of that truck?' He frowned, drew a finger across his throat, and suggested I ride on farther and camp at a church. I pursed my lips, then, reluctantly, climbed back on the bike. It was probably better to take his advice.

19

Crazy Mohammad

The truck-repair man pumped up my back tyre and gave me a bag of oranges before I rode on. Within a few minutes, being weary and unable see my way, I realised it was all too hard, so I pulled off the road, spread my sleeping bag and mattress in a culvert, and dossed down.

At some time, I was wakened by a figure leaning over me. 'Mohammad has told me I must put your bike on my truck and take you to his homestay,' he urged. Even though he said Mohammad's place was only a short drive away, I was determined to stay where I was. When I managed to persuade the man that I was okay, he bade me goodnight and drove off.

Next morning I spotted oil under the bike, closer inspection a broken pipe to the engine. I decided to chance it, and my luck held into Toudeshk, on a plateau at 2100 metres: no wonder I had been cold the night before until I had snuggled into my sleeping bag.

After a warming breakfast at Tak-Taku, its owner, Mohammad Jalali, took me to a refrigeration repair shop where a new pipe was made in no time at all. Yet again, my offer of payment was refused.

Later, while wandering in the dusty alleyways of the old part of Toudeshk, where ochre mud walls blended with a backdrop of dry, open desert, I was intrigued by an ancient domed reservoir. It seems that, during the hot summer months, as wind travels through the brick towers, (bagdirs) it cools the water, 15 metres below.

As the only roadside lodging between Isfahan and Yazd, Tak-Taku is a delight for travellers who appreciate the clean accommodation and superb home-cooked dishes provided by Mohammad and his family.

Sitting cross-legged on the floor at meal times, Mohammad would talk about previous guests, village life, and how he had come to be hosting

Roadside repairs on the road to Esfahan - Iran

Effie in Toudeshk - Iran

guests from all over the world. This is what he told me:

I was born in the historic village of Toudeshk, a camel-trading post on the old Silk Road that crosses the deserts of central Iran. When I was a child, I didn't know about any other world. I thought that everywhere was the same; that everywhere was Toudeshk. I would go to the highway to see the people passing by. While the other children played, I was always at the highway, watching.

Sometimes, especially in the winter, I would see cyclists — loaded with luggage and speaking different languages — arriving before nightfall. Sometimes they would stop and ask me something. They would always say, 'Hello', but I didn't understand 'Hello'. I didn't know who these people were, or what they were doing. I would see them going to the store to buy food and water. And then they would retreat to the middle of nowhere to sleep in tents and sleeping bags. I saw so many of them!

When I got to secondary school, the first time my English teacher said 'Hello', I jumped up like a spring and told him I'd heard this word, but I didn't know the meaning. He asked me where I'd heard it, and I answered, 'From the highway, from the mysterious cyclists'. I told him that I didn't know where any of these people came from. My teacher told me they were foreigners; that they came from other countries. I asked him why they were sleeping in tents, and he told me that it was because they didn't have a place to stay. Then my teacher started to talk about them, and other countries and cultures.

I was tired of seeing the same faces everyday — small-town syndrome! So I told my teacher that I wanted to host foreigners in my home — but I needed a key. Language was the key. He taught me conversational English. I wrote a few sentences on a piece of paper and went and waited by the highway.

People changed my name to 'Crazy Mohammad', because I would wait there for a long time, watching the road. Even during bad weather, I was there, trying to 'fish' cyclists and invite them to my house. I would ask truck and bus drivers if they'd seen any cyclists that day, and when they answered 'yes', I was happy, and would wait for them to arrive.

When they arrived, I took my piece of paper and said, 'Hello', and they all answered, 'Hello'. Finally, I had the opportunity to host one of them, and he taught me about cyclists and what they needed. I learnt much from him and others after him.

And so I finally reached my dream of running somewhere where I could meet and talk to new people. Since starting Tak-Taku Homestay, I have hosted over 3,000 people in my home. Now all the people of Toudeshk know more about foreigners and all of them can say 'Hello'! In the village I am no longer known as 'Crazy Mohammad', I am now 'Mohammad Tourist'.'

Mohammad, in his pursuit of providing a bridge between his people and the wider world, has achieved so much. Not only has he acquired a high level of English, he has a shrewd understanding of his market and he has found ways to give people what they want.

At his sister's house, Mohammad showed me rich silk rugs made by village women, and I watched traditional weaving techniques. In appreciation of his expansive hospitality, I repaired the clutch on his old Honda. When I decided to stay an extra day, he kindly gave me a night's accommodation free.

Before I left Toudeshk, I climbed a hill overlooking the town. High above the Dasht-e Kavir desert clusters of small desert flowers decorated the rocky terrain, a reminder of nature's resilience even in the harshest of climates.

Ninety-seven kilometres further on, at Isfahan, I fell under the spell of a truly beautiful city with its classic Persian architecture, and, at its heart, spanning the Zayandeh River, the stately Si-O-Seh Pol stone bridge with its 33 arches.

In Isfahan I successfully applied to extend my visa by a further month. Compared with the problems I'd had obtaining a visa to enter Iran, getting the extension was easy.

By May 2, I was on my way to Kashan. I was late getting away from the hotel because I met a Romanian couple, Laura and Adrian, who kindly offered to pass on, through Lynne, information about travel in Romania.

A steady climb took me through the mountains to the north-west. Though snow still glistened on the ranges, the desert bloomed with green tussock and orange and yellow flowers. For the first time since I arrived in Iran I put up my tent, not far from the motorway. Light rain on the roof had me leaping out of bed to put the fly on. Then the wind blew so violently I had to lean against the inside wall of the tent to prevent it from being swept away.

By dawn, the weather had cleared. I crawled from the tent aching and dog-tired. Having tried unsuccessfully to sleep in a sitting position with my legs holding down as much of the tent as they could cover, had made for a rough night and a less than promising start to the day.

Before reaching Kashan, I stopped for fuel and breakfast. There, a fellow customer insisted on paying for my meal. Either I must have looked as if I didn't have a penny to my name, as well as being sleep-deprived, or the world I was travelling in really was made up of many wonderfully generous people who just wanted me to think well of them and their country.

While searching for a hotel in Kashan, I met a man who then cycled five kilometres out of his way to direct me to one. When we arrived, it was fully booked because of the spring holiday, so I parked among hundreds of holidaying families who had congregated in a park. Everywhere on grassed median strips there were barbecues, blankets and gas cookers.

Mr Mehdi, the owner of the hamburger stand opposite the park, left his staff in charge of Effie while he took me on his motorbike to tour the old city. A highlight was the splendid Tabatabayee, one of the many magnificent merchants' houses for which Kashan is famous.

On my return to the park, a lady in a hijab from a nearby apartment approached and handed me a bowl of oranges, apples and grapes. 'Are you an American?' she asked shyly.

I set up my tent near to Mr Mehdi's hamburger stand and despite a noisy crowd camped nearby, I was soon off in the land of nod.

With only 250 kilometres to go to Tehran, I was in no hurry because Lynne wasn't due to arrive for several days. When I stopped at a roadside stall for a drink, the vendor presented me with a bag of juicy apricots. A little further on, while I waited for the bike to cool down, a doctor stopped his car to see if I had a problem. When I assured him all was fine, he opened the boot and took out a rock-melon. I couldn't refuse it, so squeezed the fragrant fruit into my pannier. At least it wasn't a watermelon!

After a problem-free day, I pulled in to a large parking area, alongside a restaurant and fuel station. The constant traffic, and people stopping to take photos and chat, made it an inconvenient campsite. As I'd ridden across the flat wasteland from Kashan, I'd seen what appeared to be a shimmering lake, and was thinking it was possibly a good place to camp. It turned out to be a dry saltpan, so, with no obvious options, I decided the big parking lot would have to do.

Next day, I found a similar, but more private spot alongside a mosque,

In Toudeshk - Iran

Ice cold night sleeping rough - Iran

tucked behind a supermarket, food outlets and fuel station. I only had 50 kilometres ride to Tehran, but I was waiting for a call from the Firouzeh Hotel, to confirm that, if I arrived earlier than expected, the room Lynne had booked would be available. Lynne was not due to arrive in Tehran for a few days, and I wanted to avoid riding around the huge city trying to find alternative accommodation. Besides, I could spend the time doing laundry and cleaning the bike.

When I went for fuel, a motorist stepped in to pay for my four litres, brushing away my protests. Then people were offering me ice cream and drinks, some even pressing money into my hand. Iranians were showing themselves to be the most generous people I'd ever met, and everyone seemed genuinely keen to make me feel welcome in their country.

We are used to tourists in Australia, but I don't think it would occur to most of us to offer presents to strangers. In Iran, maybe because foreigners are rare, I was frequently treated as a special guest.

I decided to camp beside the mosque for one more night. The hotel manager had still not returned my call and I was at a loose end. It had been a month since Lynne and I were together, and I was missing her. On reflection, staying longer in Isfahan — a city I'd enjoyed so much — might have been wiser, but I always had the urge to move on after a few days in any one place. Still, the time would not be wasted. I could spend it checking the bike, tightening anything that was loose. I had travelled 1,300 kilometres since Bam, and now would be a good time to reset Effie's inlet valves.

Travelling in foreign parts, especially when everything seems to be going far too well, one gets a sense that the luck is going to run out. Well, that morning, at a roadside parking lot, mine did. When I returned to my tent after breakfast at the nearby eatery, I saw that it had been slashed and all my belongings were gone.

20

Highway Robbery

Rooted to the spot, I tried to comprehend the scene. Apart from the long gash in the tent, nothing appeared disturbed. Then it dawned: the tent was empty. Heart pounding, head in my hands, fingers rubbing my temple. How could this have happened? So secure had I felt in Iran that never for a moment did I suspect I would be the target of thieves. Devastated, eyes casting around in a daze, I was at a loss at what to do next.

A high brick wall surrounded the parking area. I clambered on top of it to see if there were signs someone had used this route to escape. I sensed more than one person had to be involved. No sign of anyone, or my property, in the scrubby wasteland beyond. They must have arrived and left by car.

Luckily, I had the iPhone with me. I called Lynne in Lahore, where she was waiting for her Iranian visa.

'Are you alright?' she said.

'I'm fine, a bit shaken up, but I'm okay.'

'Did they steal your carnet and passport?'

'No, thank goodness, I had them on me. But the panniers, backpack and all my clothes are gone. Virtually everything I was carrying.' I didn't mention the hefty sum of money that had gone.

'Don't worry, we can replace it all when you get to Tehran,' Lynne reassured me. 'As long as you're okay, that's the main thing.'

Without the carnet, I'd have been in real trouble because it was the only way I could get the FN in and out of each country. In Iran, the customs duty was 500 per cent of the value of the bike if I couldn't prove it had entered and left the country legally.

'I'm with Ali and Akbar at a motor show,' Lynne said. 'It's really noisy here and I can't hear you very well. I'll be there in a couple of days.

Message me if you need anything. Everything will work out. Meanwhile, take care of yourself. I love you.'

I said goodbye, and returned to the supermarket, still dazed. The owner called the police, who arrived within 20 minutes, and he offered to store my bike while I went to the police station.

I did my best to make a statement. For two hours, I struggled to answer questions and fill out forms, but no one spoke English well enough for me to be understood. Confused and out of my depth, I agreed to go with the officers to police headquarters in Tehran to file a second report. Hassan, a soldier, speaking good English assured me that all my gear would be returned, but that did nothing to lessen my feeling that even being at police headquarters was a pointless exercise.

'They say they'll send for the Australian consulate and they will give you money,' Hassan said confidently.

Yeah, that's likely! I didn't have much faith in bureaucracy and, besides, this was my problem, and the fewer people involved the better. A clerk was sent out to buy me a sandwich and a cola for lunch. Later, a higher official asked the same questions again, and wrote down my contact details. The day dragged on. Finally, at 5.00 pm, I was told I could leave. By then, I was slumped in a chair: eight hours had passed since I left the supermarket, and I was shattered.

'So, how do I find my way back?' I asked, wearily.

'In a taxi,' came the indifferent reply.

'But you brought me here, and it's 50 kilometres. The least you can do is return me there. It's been a bloody waste of time and I'm too tired to care anymore.'

Hassan grudgingly agreed, but he had no idea where to take me. He resorted to phoning the first police station to find where I'd been picked up. Eventually he managed to borrow a car. After 45 minutes, we pulled into a fuel station.

'Here you are,' the soldier said confidently.

'This isn't it,' I said, peering around for something familiar. Hassan shrugged. My irritation palpable, he reluctantly went to ask for further instructions. It was another half-hour before we found the right place.

Physically and emotionally, I was drained. All of this was a result of my own stupidity, and I was furious — not at Hassan, who was doing his best to help me, but at myself. Because of everyone's cordiality, I'd let my guard down, and that was just plain dumb.

The fuel station security man insisted that I spend the night in the

Afghani janitor's quarters in the mosque complex. I could see only one bed, and wasn't about to turn its occupant out of it, so I lay down on the floor next to the bed.

Next morning, before leaving for Tehran, I wrote in my diary a list of everything that had been stolen. It included clothes, spare tubes, tyre gauge, reading glasses, camera charger, bungy cords, wet-weather gear and thermals, eating utensils, water bottles, a few odds and ends, and a number plate. I'd carried a whistle in case of emergency, and a wallet containing a small amount of cash, a N.S.W. driving license, expired credit cards and an old passport, in case I was confronted by robbers. All this, plus US$1,000, had been stowed in the bottom of my now stolen backpack — for 'safekeeping'!

I fantasised a police 'Wanted' description: 'Man wearing Pakistani topi hat, antique goggles and large red backpack full of dirty underwear, carrying two red plastic jerrycans, and pretty cool Dry Rider panniers, and flogging off spare parts for an antique Belgium motorcycle.' For all I knew, he might be found buying his mates a few drinks with his windfall cash.

I hoped karma would catch up with him/them one way or another. If my experience with the law was anything to go by, I figured it was doubtful the police would ever find the thieves. Our family home had been robbed once, and we'd had to do our own super-sleuthing to find the crims. Of course, our goods had long been disposed of before the police decided to pay a visit to those teenage crooks. I wasn't holding out much hope that the outcome would be any different this time.

21

Down, but not Out

On the short ride into Tehran, I was angry and uptight. I wanted to get my hands on the thieves and wring their necks. They'd even taken the gift of dates from Akbar's Guest House that I'd planned to share with Lynne. *Bastards!*

Chaotic traffic, battered taxis, choked roadways and confusing Persian signs were aggravating me as never before. By the time I reached the city centre, my head was thumping, perhaps, too, because I hadn't eaten all morning. When I stopped to buy breakfast and get my bearings, a crowd quickly gathered. A motorcyclist pulled alongside, professing to know the Firouzeh hotel, and offered to guide me there.

I scoffed my muffin and followed him. On the way, he stopped and asked how much I intended to pay him. It was not a good day for anyone to be rattling my chain. Coldly, I stared him in the eye — and said nothing. Looking sheepish, and realising he wasn't going to make a fast rial, he flagged down a passerby to ask for directions, then, without a word, took me straight to the hotel.

I checked in and made arrangements with the manager to store Effie at a nearby apartment building. All I wanted to do was crawl into bed, pull the covers over my head and try to forget the previous day's events. Once the bike was stowed, I locked the door to my room, took a couple of Panadols and stretched out on one of the narrow cots.

Sometimes my body felt so tired it didn't seem to matter where I bedded down for the night. In the three months I'd been on the road, I had slept on charpoys, in a tent, in a prison, in abandoned buildings, in police posts, in the odd memorable hotels or guesthouse, and in a handful of questionable establishments.

I'd shared my space with travellers, been under the stars and alone in

Bikes loaded on pickup - Iran

Lynne in Shiraz - Iran

Oil and sand - Iran

the desert, had a whole dormitory to myself, and I'd curled up in a room no bigger than a cupboard. When the urge to crash hit, I could sleep anywhere, be it a roadside culvert or under a bush. My early morning waking moments could be a glorious sunrise, a call to prayers, a cacophony of traffic horns, sometimes even a combination of all three.

This night, I was woken at 3.00 am by the racket of groaning carts overloaded with empty Sanyo crates. These were being pulled by youthful Kurdish refugees, desperate to scrape a meagre living in a less-than-welcoming community. Then the roosters got going. At the foot of snowcapped mountains, the heaving metropolis that is Tehran was stirring into its daily roared life. Knowing that I had nowhere to go, I rolled over, determined to catch a few more zeds.

I spent the next three days replacing my losses. Some purchases weren't vital, but I was disorientated and desperately needed to pick up where I'd left off.

I was in a clothing shop when my phone rang. Because I couldn't understand what was being said, I handed the phone to the manager, who spoke good English. It was the police. They told him what had happened, yet again saying that I should get the Australian diplomatic mission involved. I shook my head, and the shopkeeper seemed to empathise with my reticence to tangle with yet more officialdom.

'I am so ashamed my countrymen would do this to a traveller,' he said, and gently pushed my money back across the counter. Because of his generosity, I returned a few days later for several more items — and insisting that I pay for them.

Lynne, in headscarf, Pakistani kurta and dark glasses, was barely recognisable as she entered the hotel. Exhausted from her flight, she was struggling under the weight of her backpack and hefty suitcase. In it was not only her own gear for six months on the road, but spare tubes and spokes that would keep Effie rolling.

I bounded down the stairs and we wrapped our arms around one another. It was such a relief to hear her voice, and for her to know I was safe, if only in that moment. As we shared stories, there were brief sessions of self-recrimination and soul searching, yet, ultimately, we gratefully acknowledged that things could have been so much worse.

The theft reminded me of how tough it can be to travel alone: to cope with unexpected challenges day in, day out, and never be able to escape eyes that watch your every move. Equally, I accepted that I had chosen to challenge myself in this way, and had never been under any illusion that it was going to be easy. Much of what I'd lost wouldn't have been of use to anyone else and should probably have been discarded earlier. I remained certain nothing would be recovered. The best I could do was to lay it to rest, and move on.

Before we could make plans, Lynne was hit with bad diarrhoea. All I could do was sponge her clammy forehead between her staggering to and from the toilet. The shared restroom was down the hallway. Usually, when she went there, she was mindful to don a headscarf and ensure she was well covered. On occasion, though, getting there was more important than observing the dress code. Those times, she snuck out in a T-shirt. Days later, we noticed a closed-circuit screen at reception, realising that Lynne's sprints down the hall — minus scarf and with bare legs — could be observed by staff!

Leaving Lynne to sleep fitfully, I visited a few local attractions. In one part of the city, moneychangers stood on street corners, with open suitcases stuffed full of notes, competing noisily with one another for foreign currency.

As I was trying to negotiate a favourable exchange rate, a gust of wind blew the first few layers of notes from one man's case into the path of oncoming pedestrians. Without slowing down, passersby scooped up handfuls of money, then quickened their step as they went on their way. I looked on in amazement, wondering what had happened to their sense of fair play.

A few days later, still weak, but feeling a little more in control, Lynne dosed up on foul-tasting Flagyl, and we took a cab to the home of Behnum, a charming young guy I'd met in Yazd. He had invited us for dinner with his family, and Lynne was eager to get out of the hotel room, if only for a few hours. As we passed row upon row of luxury stores and showrooms, we realised we were seeing a more affluent side to Tehran than where we were staying. The city, bigger than I had envisaged, sprawls for miles in every direction.

The hospitality for which Iranians are renowned awaited us. Stepping through Behnum's front door, we were greeted by a beguiling aroma of freshly baked food. What a feast his mother had prepared! Bowls of nuts, sweets and crystallised fruits lay before us. Then came delicious homemade mushroom soup, baked chicken, succulent kebabs, vegetable dishes, salads and fragrant rice, and mouthwatering desserts.

Lynne, unable to eat for several days, struggled to manage more than a few mouthfuls. I, at the insistence of our hosts, stuffed myself with the most delicious food I'd had since leaving home. I was able to relax and enjoy the hospitality and forget, even for a short time, recent events.

It was enlightening to discuss many topics with such a well-educated family and their friends. One woman who had spent time in detention shared her harrowing experiences. Nevertheless, an air of optimism reigned in the room, and we saw it frequently among many other people we were to meet throughout Iran. Many young women, testing the boundaries, wear jeans and make-up, and daringly push their scarves back as far as they can.

Many rights that we in the West take for granted are still not recognised in Iran, and police keep a close eye on social behaviour. We met people who were making changes from within, and from our perspective, that seemed a good place to start.

Tehran, at 1,100 metres above sea level, has traffic comparable with that of big Indian cities. Narrow pavements are cluttered with motorcycles, whitegoods, teetering stacks of plastic pipes, exhaust fans, tyres, mobile phones… and, of course, teeming masses of pedestrians.

The tranquility of the Golestan Palace Gardens, with its lush shady avenues and ornate ponds made a welcome respite from the hustle and bustle of the city. No stay in Tehran is complete without a visit to the Central Bank of the Islamic Republic of Iran, where the Imperial Crown Jewels of Persia are kept. Renowned as the world's largest collection of gems, which included the Darya-ye-Noor diamond, emeralds, sapphires and rubies, last worn in the late 1970s, by the Shah of Iran and his wife Empress Farah.

Once Lynne was well enough to travel, we took the overnight train to Shiraz, sharing a compartment with three men. Only the youngest could speak English, and he kept himself amused practicing slang expressions he had heard on television.

I basked in the freedom to amble around Shiraz without worrying about the motorcycle, sharing with Lynne the fascinating sights — ornate mosques, stalls brimming with mountains of spices looking like desert rainbows, pistachios, dried and candied figs and oranges, anise and cinnamon. An old man, skin the colour of ripe walnuts — oblivious to passersby — sat cross-legged on the pavement weaving recycled plastic strips into brooms. And we savoured alluring smells, especially the scent of hot bread that wafts through the street as the loaves are slid out of the stone ovens on long wooden peels.

We arranged a hire car to take us to Persepolis and Necropolis, seats

Shiraz broom maker - Iran

Shiraz spice shop - Iran

Gardens - Shiraz, Iran

of ancient civilisation. We were astounded by the size and beauty of these age-old Persian ruins, about an hour's drive from Shiraz. Incredibly well preserved in the dry desert air, Persopolis is believed to have spanned an even greater empire than that of the Romans, 2500 years ago.

Karim, our chatty and informative guide, produced green tea, biscuits and fresh watermelon as we rested from the heat 10 kilometres further on beneath the rock-face crypts at Necropolis.

From Shiraz, it was a comfortable but fatiguing six-and-a-half hour bus journey to Isfahan. Lynne fell in love with the city as I had done. At the Grand Bazaar, we watched in awe as women carved fine silver filigree work, and painted lapis lazuli designs on pottery. The discovery of a shop selling old Afghani and Iranian tribal jewelry had Lynne drooling.

The cool brick bazaar was a welcome relief from the noonday sun. Walking through its entirety takes several hours. Each passageway is crowded with tiny shops. Old men beat brassware, or stamped traditional paisley designs on locally grown cotton fabric. Carpets, renowned for their intricate designs hung invitingly and the scent of spices and colourful sweets lured passersby.

A leisurely stroll through one of Isfahan's many tranquil parks took us to the Chehel Palace, where a long narrow pool reflects the slender wooden columns at the far end of a pavilion. With its breathtakingly beautiful golden honeycomb-shape ceiling, colourful frescos depicting merchants from Asia and Europe, exquisite tilework and well-preserved ceramic panels, ancient mirrors and artefacts, it's not surprising that the Palace of the Forty Columns is a UNESCO World Heritage site.

All too quickly it was time to leave Isfahan. We had checked out of our hotel and were on our way in a taxi when I discovered my iPhone was missing. I called Totia reception on Lynne's phone, and they agreed to search our room.

The phone held not only all my contact numbers, it also had music and family photos that had been of comfort to me in some of my tougher moments. My mind's eye told me exactly where I had left the phone. But it was too late to go back and check for myself when the receptionist insisted it wasn't there. We had a bus to catch. Just one more happening to put down to experience.

22

Land of Dates and Honey

The loss of my iPhone was very much on our minds as our coach rolled through the night. We arrived back in Tehran after midnight, tired and dejected. Next day, I bought a cheap phone but, with everything on it written in Persian, I struggled to operate it. At least it provided a contact number for Lynne and might be useful in an emergency.

We had arranged through Thomas of Schafer & SIS — a German air-freight and logistics services company — for two spare tyres and extra tubes to be sent to Tehran. Thomas, who was following us via my blog, told me I could pick them up from Mamoud, his cargo agent in Tehran. It was a relief to know I would once more have quality tyres when I set off for Turkey in a few days' time.

Meanwhile, with the bike still in storage, we took a bus through the highlands of northern Iran, and then on to Tonekabon, near the Caspian Sea. Here, we planned to spend a few days at an organic homestay.

On our way out of the city we passed the Shahyad Tower (Kings Memorial) in Azadi Square. Built in 1971, the stunning monument is shaped from 8,000 blocks of white marble stone. Motoring up steep and winding roads into the majestic Alborz range at 3,000 metres, we looked out at dramatic panoramas of plunging ravines and snow-dusted peaks.

We didn't find the world's largest enclosed body of water anything like our romantic and fertile minds had imagined. The Caspian lies at 28 metres below sea level, and for much of this southern stretch of coast ugly concrete buildings dominate. The black sand beach is unattractive and the heat intense. The few females on the beach, all in black burkas, must have been most uncomfortable. The men, of course, were free to strip down to their swim trunks and get into the water.

Farzin and Alejandra, owners of our homestay, built their traditional

Goat herders - Tonekabon, Iran

Desert camping - Iran

mud house (Khoone Geli) 13 kilometres inland, away from the noise and pollution. Nestled among orange trees, Khoone Geli provides a simple rural way of life, a welcome respite for the wealthy, travelling there for weekend stays. Farzin's Caspian Tours offers guided hiking excursions that pass through ancient summer villages in the mountains and valleys. In season, they are resplendent with wildflowers. In the warmer months, the Alamuti people graze flocks of goats, sheep and cows on the hillsides.

Our hosts served us homemade cheeses, breads, divine rose-petal marmalade, local honey, yoghurt, pickled garlic, olives, plump dates and the best cherry tart ever. All of this we enjoyed sitting cross-legged on the floor, a heavily burdened 'tablecloth' spread out before us.

At Mohebbi's pottery in Siyahgelchal, near Soleiman Abad, we watched three generations of one family at work. While we chatted, the matriarch of the family pressed the dough we had taken with us onto the sides of a circular shaped clay oven to be baked. It emerged hot and steaming. One of the highlights for us was the visit of a local shepherd who spent the evening entertaining us with his flute. The old man, with no formal musical knowledge, had taught himself to play the instrument while tending his flock as a boy.

To mark Farzin's birthday, we accompanied his family 200 kilometres to Masouleh, a 1,000-year-old town high in the Alborz Mountains. We drove to Rasht, then left the coast heading south to the Gasht-Rodkan Protected Area, where we stopped so that Farzin and I could climb, through the woods, hundreds of steps to the Markuh Fortress (Rud-Khan Castle). It was quite a climb to the 1,000-year-old stone watchtower, and despite my physical workouts on the bike, the climb had me breathless in no time.

An hour's drive further on stands Masouleh, a rustic collection of ancient adobe and stone houses. Their ornately carved and latticed wooden windows contrast sharply with the bright yellow clay exteriors of the houses. Packed dried leaves insulate the houses against the freezing winters. Potted geraniums adorn the balconies, and grapevines offer shade in the courtyards where women sit chatting and sipping hot sweet tea while they knit colourful socks to sell to tourists. Vehicles are unable to enter Masouleh's narrow streets and access to accommodation is up steep stairs.

The town has many teahouses, known as chaykhunes; and a bustling bazaar that sells handicrafts, copperware, kilims made from goat's hair, traditional shoes, knives, sweets, pastries and cakes. Masouleh —

surrounded by forests in which are many springs, rivers and waterfalls — is often shrouded in dense fog. Next day, after visiting the Guilan Rural Heritage Farm, renowned for its thatched, wood and mud dwellings, we farewelled our friends and boarded the coach back to Tehran.

Once again Lynne and I were about to go our separate ways. While I was collecting Effie from storage and setting out for the Turkish border, Lynne was waking up in Lebanon.

It had been good to have a break from riding, to put recent events from my mind and enjoy Lynne's company. Now I was hungry for the next stage. As soon as I got on the bike, I was acutely aware that my couple of weeks off the road had turned my arse to putty.

Traffic on the freeway was manic: a stop-start frenzy of vehicles that bunched up from three lanes into five, and made the endless line of trucks look like a centipede with neither head nor tail. It got to be such a squeeze at times that I was able to make more progress by getting out of it all and pushing the bike along the edge of the road. After eight hours, I'd covered only 220 kilometres.

Effie, to her credit, was running well. The replacement luggage I'd bought in Tehran was not a patch on the stolen Dry Rider panniers, but was doing its job, and the Iranian-made equivalents had been a darned sight cheaper.

On 31st May, setting off before dawn, within a few hours I was riding under a sea of blue marked only with the odd sudsy cloud. As the day rolled on, steady inclines became more frequent, each one telling me a bike seizure was imminent. When I stopped to allow Effie to cool, I heard Lynne trying to call me, but couldn't connect with her because I still couldn't work the new phone.

Adobe villages, blending into the landscape, punctuated my desert ride, only the sky-blue doors of the flat-roofed homes allowing me to pick them out from the surrounding hills. Their occupants keep sundried cakes of dung in hive-shaped mounds in front of their homes, and sometimes on the medium strip on the highway. The dung, each piece resembling a quoit, is the only fuel available in a treeless world.

Next day, it again dawned clear. I'd chosen a reliable time of year to travel, but was still expecting to meet a little rain now and then. I hadn't used my wet-weather gear since leaving Nepal, four months before.

As the sun dipped behind the mountains, the landscape turned to rich ochre. And the temperature dropped so sharply my thermals offered little resistance to the cold, though I wouldn't have been without them.

My freshly repaired tent stood incongruously, like an orange beacon, alongside a flock of chocolate-brown sheep. Being in a tent induces a cosy sense of security: once the zip is closed, the outside world disappears and I was alone with my thoughts. A sense of peace descends, and I feel I have been rescued from the bedlam of the everyday.

Leaving at sunrise, I approached Tabriz across the semi-arid desert alive with rolling tumbleweeds. Gradually, this gave way to a sprawling metropolis with very few signs in English. I chose to keep moving westward, travelling around the outskirts of the city. I guessed Tabriz had its share of tourist attractions, but my sights were now set on my next country, Turkey, where I knew new adventures awaited me.

With the desert disappearing behind me, and cultivated valleys ahead, it was easy riding as I closed in on the border. The temperature began to plummet, and I was grateful for a parting gift of leather gloves from Mickey, an Iranian motorcyclist who had stored Effie while Lynne and I were sightseeing. Snow-covered Mt Ararat grew closer, little Ararat at her side. I stopped to photograph this awe-inspiring sight. Not so impressive was the road which was visibly deteriorating as I got nearer to the border.

I crawled past a long stream of vehicles, all waiting to go through customs. One of the few benefits of being on a bike was being able to go to the front of the queue. Gravel, potholes and an ever-steepening climb had me struggling. By the time I reached the border post, at the top of the hill, perspiration was running down my back, and I could barely catch my breath.

That's when hordes of moneychangers surrounded me, pushing and shoving and calling, 'My friend, my friend.' As I was about to enter the first customs building one of the more aggressive touts grabbed my documents, claiming I was at the wrong office.

'I can do it for you, Mister, for only 30 euros.'

'Piss off, I wasn't born yesterday.'

'Well, 20 then.'

Totally exhausted, and in no mood for this, I took his photo before he scurried off, my intent being to identify who had taken my carnet if it never came back. Suddenly, three burly policemen grabbed me, insisting I was in a prohibited area. One demanded my camera. Thinking quickly, I turned the button to a different setting so that, when they looked, there was no photo showing either the tout or the border-post building. *Phew!*

On the road from Tabriz to the border - Iran

From Tabriz to the border - Iran

I remembered from travelling through South America how necessary it is to get in the right mindset before crossing a border. Procedures can be lengthy and often frustrating, especially when you don't speak the language. Still, they are unavoidable obstacles for those who embark on international overland journeys, and they do add to the excitement. Once through a border post, it is a relief to have all the right boxes ticked and paperwork stamped, and to know everything is in order. Hopefully, my brush with the police wouldn't be to my detriment. I crossed my fingers and waited.

23

A Word of Warning

Once through Iranian customs, I pushed the bike 100 metres uphill across the demarcation zone to the Turkish control post. Totally spent, I sought refuge from the hot sun under an awning, and ate the chocolates and biscuits I'd bought with my last remaining Iranian rials. Trucks on the Turkish side, as they did across the border, snaked back about five kilometres, the drivers standing about drinking and smoking, killing time as they awaited vehicle inspection.

It was a pleasant change not to be pestered by touts. Turkish immigration officials speedily processed my paperwork and took me across the road to the insurance office. The visa to enter Turkey cost me US$20 and the bike insurance, which I doubted would be honoured, another $30. The insurance clerk apologised that his computer could only date vehicles back 45 years, and there was no category for bikes of Effie's vintage. The Turkish import document, stating I was riding a 1970 FN, was wildly inaccurate: the FN factory had ceased motorcycle production in the '60s. I could only hope this would not create a problem somewhere down the track.

Ahead, the road was well sealed and, pleasingly, mostly downhill. Mid-afternoon, I pulled into a market on the outskirts of Dogubayazit to get my bearings. The owner of a hamburger shop beckoned me in, insisting I have the crusty bread, tomatoes and cucumbers he'd been about to enjoy. Gratefully, I tucked into my first real meal for the day.

He then offered to keep an eye on Effie while I walked to the Hotel Ararat. As usual, I had been getting directions for every which way, so I'd decided it was easier to leave the bike and walk. Once I'd booked in, it was another tiring two kilometre walk back to pick up the bike and ride it to the Ararat, where I was instructed to park in the hotel's reception area. I wondered what other guests thought about a motorcycle inside the hotel!

As always, I revelled in the luxury of a steaming shower. Then I scrubbed my filthy gear clean before tracking down a SIM card outlet. After waiting two hours for my new card to be activated I was told it wouldn't work until the next day, so I insisted on a refund and went in search of a Vodaphone card.

After four days of riding 940 kilometres from Tehran, I relished the prospect of stretching my legs. However, deciding that the 10 kilometre hike to the Ishak Pasa Palace was a bit further than I wanted to walk, I hitched a ride. When I got there, I found it closed for renovation. Disappointed, I started the long walk back, but got a lift from the first passing motorist. No one, it seemed, was reluctant to pick up strangers.

That evening, I had a beer and swapped a few yarns with a Swedish motorcyclist on the rooftop terrace with its spectacular view of Mount Ararat.

Effie was in sore need of a service. For a start, she had two collapsed inlet-valve springs, which had to be replaced before we got under way again. I had hoped to find a few items waiting for me at the hotel, including maps and a much needed tyre pump, but they hadn't arrived, so I had to ride on without them.

When I went to pay for my accommodation, the manager first said he would reduce my bill by 50 percent, then suddenly declared that he had 'instructions' from Istanbul' not to charge me. I could only presume the 'instructions' came from the Istanbul Bisiklet Motosiklet Ihtisas Kulubu, (Istanbul Cycling Biking Specialty Club Association) who were active in assisting international motorcyclists. If so, this totally unexpected gesture was much appreciated.

On June 5, I set out for Lake Van, having been informed by Klaus and Susie, a motorcycling couple I'd met at the hotel, that the roads were fine. Over the top of the first hill, I stopped for ice cream at a roadside stall, where Klaus and Susie caught up with me. When we got started again, they rode alongside me taking photographs, then, with a wave, they headed off. What they'd forgotten to mention was just how steep the hills were about to become.

It soon became apparent the long climbs were too much for Effie. For modern bikes, mountains are part of the magic. The thrill of racing up or down them is a heady sensation. Now, I had to mentally brace myself for each one. Increasingly, I had to get off and push, and the more often I did, the more exhausted I became.

I was hunched over the bike — trying to regain my breath after a spell of pushing — when a truck stopped. The driver didn't speak English, but he could see I needed a hand. Several times he helped me push, before deciding it would be better to give me a tow.

It was a suggestion that didn't appeal to me. I knew full well that most drivers have no idea how to safely tow another vehicle, especially a motorcycle. I had visions of being splattered on the back of his truck, so I declined the offer. But, after several more pushing sessions, and with both of us on the verge of collapse, I relented.

We tied a short rope to the back of the truck and looped it around Effie's handlebars, with me holding the end of the rope in case a quick release was necessary. The driver started off gently enough, easing the truck into the next gear without the rope snatching. But, as he increased speed, I found myself out of my comfort zone. So I let go of the rope and cruised past him until, once again, it became too steep for Effie to cope.

We did this Turkish rope trick half-a-dozen times until we reached the highest point. Although we had barely exchanged more than a few words, we had shared a sense of camaraderie for about an hour. The driver would take no payment: we simply shook hands and he drove away. At times like that, I had to admit to myself that, without the help of strangers, I probably could never have made it on my own.

Soon the road levelled out, and I rode on comfortably to Van, site of the biggest lake in Turkey, and so saline that most of it doesn't freeze over in winter. With several restaurants and bars, it was a good place to set up my tent. Groups of people were picnicking in small rotundas on the lakeshore, and soon one family invited me to share their lunch of potato salad, bread, chicken and fruit. Then, when they left, another family arrived and offered me more food. Not wanting to offend, I accepted a plate of homemade kebabs, bread rolls and a drink. Two meals in one day was a luxury. The night before I'd only eaten a tin of peas.

Before I bedded down, Lynne called from Lebanon. She had received a message from Istanbul advising that I avoid the Van area 'for security reasons', suggesting it would be safer to follow the northern coastal route. Lynne called again moments later after hearing that a tourist, travelling by bus, had been kidnapped somewhere not far from where I was. This was confirmed by an email she had received from Alison, from Nomad Tours, who arranges homestays in south-east Turkey.

Alison wrote to Lynne: 'My advice would be general, and it would be things like avoiding travelling at night, or even dusk, and making sure that the road has other users on it. If your husband finds himself on an empty road, he should pull over to a service station, or even stop near a few houses and wait and join a stream of traffic. This means that, if anything does happen, the security forces will know about it. The British man who was kidnapped last week was taken in broad daylight in front of other people, but released quickly afterwards as soon as the security forces became involved. If he (Ron) should find himself in the Sanliurfa area, please get him to get in touch.'

'How about you take the northern route to Elazig?' Lynne suggested. 'That area is meant to be safer.'

'Don't worry, I'll be fine,' I assured her. No point in mentioning I was already in the heart of the zone she was worried about, or that I had no intention of backtracking, especially when I thought of those horrendous hills. I turned in for the night, grateful for the solitude and a velvet sky strewn with stars.

The next day began routinely enough, but soon turned into a harrowing ride, tougher than most. I had to push Effie for at least five kilometres through a series of steady inclines, stopping every few metres to regain my breath. I'd travelled only 60 kilometres by mid-day.

Dog-tired, I conceded defeat and decided to make camp early, determined to be fresh for an early start next day. Desperate to kick off my boots and rest, I began looking for a suitable campsite.

At the crest of an interminable hill, a broad meadow stretched out invitingly, the track to it rocky and unstable. I dismounted and heaved the bike the final 20 metres.

Had I an inkling of what the next eight hours would bring, I would have hightailed it out of there faster than a hare in a hat. Ah, the beauty of hindsight!

24

Staring Down the Barrel

A line of wind-bent trees provided a sheltered campsite, and sheep grazed nearby, their scruffy coats matted with burrs. The occupants of half-a-dozen cars lounged about enjoying a picnic. They were Roma, the true disenfranchised.

I'd finished pitching my tent when several of them wandered over.

'Here, eat, please,' one insisted, offering a large plate of stew and a mound of crusty bread. I accepted gratefully, tucking into the tasty meal as the visitors grilled me about my travels.

'Are you running away from your marriage?' one man asked.

I grinned and shook my head, 'No, I'm not. My wife is travelling on her own and we're meeting up again in Istanbul.'

Several doe-eyed children peered out from behind their mothers' skirts, while the adults discussed the pros and cons of such an odyssey, before offering me advice.

'Be careful, cobras,' an older man cautioned, his leathery eyes staring intently into mine. I hadn't seen any snakes; I didn't even know reptiles existed in the country. The gypsy, genuinely concerned, repeated his warning.

'I'll be on my guard,' I promised him, picturing myself searching the sleeping bag by torchlight for creepy-crawlies.

The group wandered off, leaving me to mop up the rich gravy with the last slabs of bread. When I returned the plate and offered my thanks, I noticed cookers set up and ample food to feed an army. I got the impression the Roma intended staying overnight. Although I enjoyed my own company, especially at the end of a tough day, having families nearby was reassuring. But leave they did, tooting their horns and waving as they went.

Dogubayazit region - Turkey

Mt Ararat - Turkey

Soon afterwards, two local lads appeared. I could see their village beyond the trees, to the south: a small, isolated settlement about a kilometre off the Diyarbakir road, where shepherds and subsistence farmers eked out a meagre living. The brasher of the two, strode into the campsite with a swagger. His young ally followed closely behind.

I was surprised, though, not unduly concerned — people often stopped by to check me out. Instead of greeting me, they headed straight for my veteran motorcycle. One boy stepped on the pedal, threatening to topple the bike. Exhausted from the day's ride, my patience was being sorely tested and I had a growing sense of foreboding.

'No, don't touch, it's very old,' I said, forcing him back. The boy's jaw tightened. To lighten the mood, I gestured as to how each part of the machine worked. Instead of paying attention, the pair ferreted through my rucksack and toolbag.

The situation didn't bode well. I shooed them away and hurriedly secured the open panniers, anxious to keep my belongings intact. When I turned my back, they unzipped the tent and one boy crawled inside. I'd grown used to the natural curiosity of onlookers, but this cocky kid was more audacious than most.

'Hey, get out of there,' I growled. When the little bugger began rummaging through my gear I dragged him out and bellowed, 'PISS OFF!'

We tussled, and I forced one arm up behind his back. He winced and glared at me, muttering in Turkish. The lad was wiry and quick on his feet, but I wasn't about to let my age stand in the way of kicking his arse if necessary. I stood my ground. Despite us not sharing a common language, I made it clear I didn't appreciate his behaviour. Our eyes locked, each sizing up the other. When I released his arm and shoved him away, he shrugged and sauntered over to where his friend stood looking on.

For a moment they huddled together, then they were darting this way and that, all the while exchanging knowing looks and giggling. They clearly had an agenda, and I hoped my gut feeling was wrong. Any rational person would have got back on the motorcycle and kept riding, but I was dead on my feet and clearly wasn't thinking straight. Besides, these were just kids who, I thought, would probably lose interest before too long.

In an effort to distract them away from my possessions, I made a show of taking photographs of the pair posing with the bike. This diversion didn't hold their attention for long. Soon they were back delving into my bags. I rested my head in my hands, closed my eyes and rubbed an aching temple.

When I looked up, the delinquents were sprinting back across the field. I'd been right. They were bored and had decided to head home. I sighed with relief and returned to stowing my gear in the tent.

But, an hour later they were back, this time with a scrawny friend in tow. All wore shabby trousers and frayed open-neck shirts; their bare feet were cracked and grimy. The leader's intense dark eyes, bony features and shock of unruly black hair were discomforting. So too was the shotgun slung over his shoulder. Although there was no meanness about his looks, I felt a gnawing sense of foreboding. Was the gun a display of machismo or were the boys simply on their way to hunt local game?

The new sidekick's boyish face disguised a sly, tough interior. He stared at me intently and spoke in a low tone. With my command of the Turkish language limited to only a few words, making conversion was virtually impossible. But, when I thought I heard the word, *para* (money) mentioned, I realised their objective: it wasn't rabbits they were after.

The older boy moved deliberately, his weapon conspicuous. As he drew a bead on this and that, I tried to appear nonchalant, but a hamster was spinning around inside my ribcage.

The youngest, and most affable of the trio — seemingly uninterested in his friend's activities — flopped on the grass alongside me, doing his damnedest to hold a conversation.

Maybe he was trying to explain that I was on private property and couldn't spend the night there, or was he was prattling on about me being a crazy old git who deserved to be robbed?

The newcomer sat nearby, flicking a cigarette lighter, and trying to ignite small tufts of grass. The sparks flared, chasing one another momentarily before fizzling out. *Thank God.* I didn't need a bloody grass fire with two cans of petrol within spitting distance. The reckless act didn't go unnoticed.

'ARHHHH!' The arsonist cowered, one arm raised to shield himself from the ringleader's fist. The pair no doubt shared a troubled history. I averted my eyes, trying to focus on what I should do. Perhaps now was a good time to abandon the campsite before anything more dangerous occurred. My mouth was dry, and I begged the pounding in my head to stop.

My water bottle lay inches away, but before I could reach for it, a flash caught my peripheral vision, and I looked up. An icy shiver trickled down my spine. One minute the bully was threatening his friend; the next he stood pointing the shotgun at my temple.

'*PARA*,' my assailant spat. '*PARA, PARA*.' His finger teased the trigger.

'Nothing, I've got nothing,' I insisted, 'No money … see.'

I patted my pockets, trusting that the pouch around my neck stayed hidden. Memories of the robbery in Iran came flooding back. I should have anticipated this and had a small amount of cash at the ready. But it was too late now for that. The boy tossed me a look of contempt.

Goading him didn't seem wise, but showing signs of vulnerability wouldn't earn me brownie points either. I tried to remain calm, testing his mettle against mine. The pressure of the barrels tattooed their mark, like the keen eyes of an owl, on my forehead.

There was no epiphany, no lightbulb moment when my life flashed before me. My view on death had always been pragmatic — but I'd never faced a situation like this before.

An ache in my groin intensified. I wanted to raise my arm and ask to be excused. Instead, my hands stayed clenched, palms moist.

Nothing moved. Even the wind held its breath.

Being towed - Turkey

Camping - Turkey

25

In the Lap of the Gods

The Roma had warned me about cobras in the area. Had they meant the reptilian variety, or were they warning me to be wary of human 'cobras'? When the boys appeared for the second time — this time three of them — the mood went from idle curiosity to menacing: the barrel of a shotgun was nuzzling the middle of my temple. No longer was I in control. The distance between me and those that I loved, and the very fragility of life, flashed through my mind.

In recent weeks, there had been fire bombings in Gilgit, and an aid worker had been beheaded in Quetta — both places I'd recently spent time in. And, only yesterday I'd learned of a kidnapping not far from where I was. How foolish had I been not to follow the advice I'd been given?

Maybe I'd been too quick to give the lad a push when I found him rummaging in my tent on his first visit. He'd resisted, so I'd twisted his arm to get him out. From his swagger, it was obvious he was the ringleader, and I had shown him up in front of his mate. So he was likely to be resentful and felt he had a score to settle, even though I was the one who should have been aggrieved.

The robbery in Iran had left me sick and angry for days. I didn't want to have that happen again. Yet now I was staring along the barrel of a gun.

Lynne was already in Istanbul: so close, yet a world away. Was everything about to change for her too? I shuddered, trying to push away the 'what-ifs'.

Although we'd discussed the possibility of something awful happening, it wasn't foremost in our minds. We were realistic enough to know that any adventure carries its share of risk. Simply walking through King's

Cross on a Saturday night you can be king-hit by a drunken thug. Yet few ever plan for, or even expect, such horrors to happen. I imagine young men going to war also believe nothing will happen to them, that they'll return safe and sound. But many don't.

It seemed like an eternity. I stayed still. The muzzle still pressed on my temple. Then it was gone. The shoulders of the teenager menacing me relaxed, and his grip on the weapon lightened. He smirked. In a slow, as if rehearsed movement, he lowered the shotgun. Arrogantly, he turned and sauntered off towards his mates, a string of expletives trailing behind him.

Giddy with relief, I sank to the ground, rubbing my temple, where only seconds before, the gun had been pressed. Was it all a bluff? Would he have had the balls to pull the trigger? Or was this a sick joke the boys had concocted between them?

But their fun wasn't over … not yet. This time it was my tent and gear that had their attention. Impatiently, they sought to uncover a hidden stash. With the three of them to watch, I was all at sea. I wanted to beat the living crap out of them, but wasn't game enough to provoke another attack. Instead, I did my best to keep my belongings that mattered most, and myself together. Apart from US dollars and local currency in a leather pouch around my neck, I didn't have anything of material value, only my passport and carnet that I knew would be difficult, if not impossible to replace.

I was concerned that when they didn't find what they were looking for, they would guess it was hidden on my person. And, if I handed it over — or didn't — what then? How desperate was this ragtag bunch of miscreants? I wished they'd just disappear back to their sad, miserable lives and leave me alone.

But I was alone. I was alone, angry, and vulnerable.

I could hear Lynne now, chiding me for not listening to my intuition. A self-confessed skeptic, Lynne has the gut instinct of a Rottweiler when she sees injustice. Once in Sydney, she chased after a robber, grabbed the wallet he had just stolen and returned it to its unsuspecting owner. I hadn't even noticed — as we walked behind the victim — the boy slide his hand into the man's back pocket and make off with it. If Lynne were here, what would she have done? Maybe she would have chased the boys away at the outset, or, on the other hand, her impulsive nature could have landed us both in even more hot water.

But this was no place for either of us to be. Not here in Diyabakir.

When a line is drawn in the sand, how much do we control the outcome? Is it in the lap of the gods, or in the hands of the assailant with a gun?

The tent — too small for more than two people — was in disarray and the boys appeared to be arguing. I stood helplessly by, too traumatised to care much about their quarrel.

Finally, with the sky fading to as dark as my mood, the trio gave up poking around. Without another glance in my direction, they slunk off across the field and disappeared into the shadows.

In a last act of defiance, they launched a barrage of rocks, a few striking the tent. I hurled a few back, hoping like hell they would reach their mark and clobber the little bastards. They all fell short. Tired after a harrowing slog on the road, I barely had the energy to toss a marshmallow, let alone a rock.

My shirt felt damp and with it came a discernible odour. I started shaking. Fatigue had already been crowding in on me, but I was afraid to sleep, expected at any moment to hear voices. Nothing. All I could hear was the sound of the wind in the trees.

I sank to the ground and held my knees. The throbbing behind my eyes refused to stop. Each time my head slumped on my chest, it jerked back up. At last, unable to stave off exhaustion, I fell in a heap on my sleeping bag, and into a madman's dreams.

26

Back on Track

Well before first light, I woke. Jumpy and still dog-tired, I crammed the sleeping bag and tent into the stuff-bag and stumbled back to the main road, anxious to be on my way as quickly possible. My head was swirling in an ocean of fog, and I was burdened by a melancholy that was to make the morning's ride even more grueling than usual. And, because she had missed her morning service, Effie was running rough, which added to my unease.

It was still dark, and I could barely see more than a few metres. Fortunately, there was no traffic. As the sun's first rays lit the sky, I pulled to the side of the road and began work on the bike. Normally, loss of engine power is because a valve spring has collapsed and the valve hangs open. This time, oil had cooked on two of the inlet-valve stems and they'd seized closed. I cleaned the gum off with petrol and a fine file, and re-assembled them. It was good to have something to take my mind off the events of the day before.

An hour or so later, I finally felt comfortable enough to stop for breakfast. In the restaurant, I erased the campsite images I'd captured the day before from my camera. And, desperate to reset my internal compass, I decided not to record that horror episode in my diary. Although it had shaken me more than I cared to admit, I was determined a bunch of hoodlums wouldn't change the way I viewed the world; nor would it prevent me from achieving my goal. But I certainly had no sense of exhilaration. It was simply time to get on with it.

The day, and I, got better as it went. I called it quits after 140 kilometres, the terrain had been hilly enough to force me to pedal frequently, but there had been no pushing. Again I camped, mindful to keep well out of sight and, hopefully, out of harm's way.

Next day, I was flying: 150 kilometres before lunch, including pedalling up three hills and pushing up one. Life was looking up! My map told me Elazig, where I had hoped to find a hotel, was a fair way off the main road, so I decided to take the road to Malatya instead.

Another terrifying couple of moments lay ahead. Two huge, wild dogs, the size of Saint Bernards, came hurtling towards me, barking wildly. They ran alongside, their jaws snapping at the bike; their eyes crazed. I pedalled as if my life depended on it, barely escaping their frenzied efforts to tear my leg off. I'd seen a few dead dogs on the road that had possibly tangled with vehicles much larger than mine.

When the dogs and their barking had faded into the distance I stopped, and leaned back in the saddle to catch my breath. I'd had a close call with the vicious beasts and hoped I wouldn't encounter any more.

But, farther on, as I ambled around the back of a building for a piss, I noticed a huge mongrel asleep a few metres away. With heart in mouth, I tried not to trip as I hotfooted it, and then pedalled Effie furiously, praying I'd be well gone before the dog woke and caught my scent. That piss could wait.

June 9 is our son Mark's birthday. A week later it is daughter Nikki's turn to celebrate. So, on Mark's birthday, I raised my water bottle and toasted them both — hopes high that we would all see each other again.

What had happened three days before had been unnerving, but I knew I had to put it to rest, and bury it beneath all my memories of the kindnesses and heartfelt generosity that had been extended to me by most people I'd met since leaving Nepal.

Now something new was on my mind: a high-pitched noise from the rear. It happened as the day drew to a close, and I was coasting down a particularly long hill. The light was almost gone and it was too late to do anything until morning. As part of my regular maintenance, I religiously packed fresh grease into the crown wheel, so it had to be something else in the driveline that was causing the noise.

At first light I removed the back wheel, pulled the crown wheel and pinion apart, and repacked the pinion bearing with grease. It was several hours before I was able to drive away from the Hotel Bezginier, where I'd spent the night.

Cresting more hills than I cared to count, I only managed 120 kilometres before camping well after sundown. My oil-stained, grimy cargo pants and shirt clung to a bone-weary body. How much longer could I keep this up? Mile after mile, hour after hour, day after day, the hills were relentless. Just one moment of glee: Effie, on her second wind, actually passed a truck!

The next two days were just as gruelling, each hill seemingly steeper than the last. One had a 10 percent gradient! On some climbs I only managed to ride part of the way before my valiant little bike slowed to a halt. Wherever I could find a run-off I parked to let the engine cool. Then I took off again, pedalling as hard as I could. One tactic to keep up momentum was to zigzag, always on the lookout for traffic behind. It was a dangerous game and not always successful. When we didn't quite make it up an incline, I was forced to roll back to the runoff I'd just left, let the engine cool, then try a different tactic.

I'd naively thought the mountains of Nepal would be the toughest, and that once I'd conquered these, I would manage the rest without too much effort. But, I hadn't counted on the toll the journey was taking on my body. Every day I had to will myself to get back on the bike. And each time I saw another hill, I approached it with dreaded resignation.

On especially steep hills, I would push Effie for 20 paces before stopping and resting the pedal on my shin to prevent the bike rolling backward. I'd stand there, telling myself I'd do another 20 steps as soon as the next truck came by, secretly hoping one never would. Then a truck would pass and I'd force myself on another 20 paces.

Although the road condition was good, heavy traffic had swept gravel to the edges. When I leaned the bike against a signpost on a gradient, she slipped over, oil and petrol spilling out. Effie lay there, defeated. I knew how she felt. I propped her upright before lying down in the culvert. I knew I must go on. But just at that moment, there was no way I could.

It would have made life easier if the FN had come with a side-stand. When the bike was fully loaded it was impossible to put down the main stand, forcing me to either hold Effie while stationary, or find something to rest her against.

As I lay there, steaming with sweat, the mobile rang. Lynne's voice was manna from heaven. My throat tightened, I wiped my eyes. I sensed Lynne was beside me, empathising with me in acknowledgement of just how hard it was — physically, mentally, emotionally. She knew from experience full well how it felt. We'd spent three years riding from Alaska to Brazil in the mid-1980s, a total of 200,000 kilometres. There were times on that journey when I would happily have turned back. But knowing what shit was behind us, and not knowing what lay ahead, always helped put our circumstances back into perspective.

It could be worse ahead. But it could also be better. My view of the world from that culvert, and Lynne on the line, told me this was one of those times. Just give me a moment, and I'll be on my way!

Taking off at sunrise - Cappadocia, Turkey

Orange grove - Turkey

27

Turkish Delight

A deep breath, and I told Lynne I'd see her at our next meeting place, Cappadocia, to were she was about to take an overnight bus from Istanbul. We were looking forward to a few days R&R, me especially.

I got out of the culvert, changed the carburettor jet to a larger size to increase Effie's power, and pressed on. At the top of each hill, I felt a mix of relief and triumph. And when people wondered about Effie's horsepower, I'd say, 'Four, but two are sleeping.'

Once out of the hills, I stopped to remove my long-sleeved shirt. It felt good to let the breeze touch my skin, but in no time I realised my mistake: I was quickly sunburnt. Now halfway across Turkey I had covered 8,000 kilometres since leaving Nepal.

The back tyre was due for a change, and I had a good-quality one from Europe that would give me plenty of rubber between bike and tarmac. Effie was purring now that I'd fixed the drive-shaft bearing problem. I'd keep that bearing well-greased from now on.

Despite the difficulties, the loneliness, and sheer exhaustion at times, I felt chuffed to have made it this far. I never doubted I could, though there were occasions when I wondered why I was doing something so insane. It only took the flat open road for my elation to rise. In those moments, I would think back to when I'd been making parts for the FN on my lathe, all the while dreaming of what it would be like to ride her back to Belgium. Now I knew — and the feeling was sweet. I'd seen only a handful of foreign motorcyclists in Turkey, most not stopping. They were high on their own adventures, and good luck to them. We each live our own dreams.

At Göreme a welcome destination, a bystander helped me push the bike up a steep and narrow lane to the Panoramic Cave Pension, where the hosts greeted me warmly. 'Welcome,' they beamed, and allowed me to park Effie out of the sun under their covered entrance.

Once I'd scrubbed up and changed my soiled clothing, I fitted the new Ensign tyre and heavy-duty tube on the rear wheel. It took me three hours to install it correctly because the thick rubber was difficult to manoeuvre over the rim, and, having a beaded edge, the tyre had to be in exactly the right position. It looked so much better than the Deestone it had replaced. I borrowed a foot pump to inflate it, my handy tyre inflator having been stolen in Iran.

From my vantage point, the topmost of the carved-out rooms in the tallest of the pension's chimney rocks, I had views over the town. The hotel was aptly named. Lynne wouldn't have been able to manage the stairs there, so when she arrived next day I joined her at the Gerdis Evi Hotel, where access was easier. Once again I was relishing hot showers, clean laundry, and sandals instead of boots. With a comfortable bed and tasty meals as bonuses my world was back to the way I liked it.

'How was everything?' Lynne asked. 'Any problems?'

'No, nothing major,' I said with a shrug. 'Just too many bloody steep hills.'

That last part at least was true, but she already knew that. There seemed little point in telling her the whole story — well, not then. I didn't want her worrying unnecessarily. So often through life, I put things out of mind and got on with doing what needed to be done. My generation of men is so conditioned to be stoic, and not share our feelings; and it doesn't come easy to fall apart, even when that might be the most natural thing to do. I wasn't about to break the mould — at least, not yet.

'You sounded knackered on the phone, you poor thing,' said Lynne.

'I didn't think I could make it at one stage,' I admitted, and told her how I'd been counting out the 20 steps, then resting, before doing it all over again — like forever!

'How do you feel now? Do you want to continue, or take some time out? There's no rush.'

'No, I'm fine, it's easy from here on,' I said, conveniently overlooking the fact that I still had to cross Europe's towering ranges. I knew that wouldn't be easy, but somehow it didn't seem to matter. I was over halfway, and nothing was going to stop me making it to Belgium.

I was relieved to hear Lynne say, that despite her original intention, she had not crossed the Lebanese border into Syria. Tensions had escalated and travellers were being cautioned to stay away. Mind you, I was a good one to talk — I rarely took notice of warnings.

Lynne had arranged her accommodation in Damascus over the Internet, and had spoken frequently to her host on Skype, who assured her that the city was safe … at least for now. Travelling by bus was advisable only during daylight hours. None of this deterred Lynne. She was keen to visit having studied Syria's rich and colorful history, but it wasn't to be.

Beirut, Lynne said, had proved disappointing. In a sprawling city, with hundreds of clubs, bars, restaurants and cafés, she was constantly woken in the early hours of the morning by young men in their Porches, BMWs and Mercedes, careering through the streets, music blaring and their horns tooting. The city was living up to its name as the nightlife capital of the Middle East.

Staff at the hotel acted aloof. Men at the airport were pushy and moneychangers barely raised a smile. Lynne had found this surprising, as Lebanese are renowned for their hospitality. She had been looking forward to visiting 'Paris of the East', but the analogy was hard to spot. The trees, for which the city was famous, had all but disappeared, and the charm of old Beirut was buried under cement and towering apartment blocks.

Only the enthusiastic staff in a backstreet restaurant — one with green tablecloths and red plastic chairs — were friendly. The owner, the chef, and several regulars had relatives in Australia. They spoke of Western Sydney and North Melbourne as if they knew them intimately, and boasted that former National Rugby League player Benny Elias and Hazem El Masri of the Canterbury Bulldogs had both been born in Lebanon.

'These guys knew a whole lot more about Australia than I did!' Lynne laughed.

Each evening, despite Lynne's protests, the restaurant owner took great delight in serving her copious amounts of food: tabbouleh, filo pastry filled with spiced mince and pine nuts, hummus topped with sweet paprika and flat-leaf parsley, spinach triangles, torpedo-shaped kibbeh, crispy-skinned fish with sumac, and fattoush — a summer salad. Pillows of warm bread kept reappearing, as if one plateful wasn't sufficient.

My mouth watered; I could taste it all. They say you can tell a lot about a country by its food. The daily banquet and the people who served it, said Lynne, more than made up for any indifference she encountered on the street.

When she tried to find the Syrian Embassy to obtain a visa no one, it seemed, could direct her. The embassy phone number was never answered and there was no listed address, only a district. Taxi drivers were no help.

'In the end, I just booked a flight to Turkey,' Lynne sighed. 'Otherwise, I might still be there looking.'

In Beirut, a few months later, a car bomb would kill eight people, and injure 78, a grim reminder of the country's unresolved issues.

Over the next few days we spent hours updating the blog and writing replies to interested followers. Readers were astonished that Effie was still going. I was surprised too, but I wasn't going to admit it. According to the papers issued at the border, I was riding a 1970 FN. There were times when I wished that was true!

Göreme, a place of fascinating scenery, has plenty to offer visitors. Its semi-arid terrain is made up of curious geological formations, many with the appearance of mushroom-like chimneys. A short walk from town, the open-air museum is a collection of odd-shaped volcanic ash buildings, each featuring carved-out rooms and windows; and the walls and ceiling of a small church are boldly decorated with colourful frescos.

Before dawn one morning, we took a hot-air balloon flight over the valley. What a spectacular ride! As our Butterfly Balloon gently lifted off, a fascinating panorama unfolded before us. Here and there, a patchwork of orange groves in which, around each tree, tractor tines had drawn fascinating swirls, ladders and ribbing into the mocha-toned earth.

A group of journalists and television cameramen arrived at the hotel to interview me. How did I like Turkey? What troubles had I encountered? I focused only on the hardships of riding rather than talk about my recent 'incident'. I regarded that as still too raw, and yet to be personally addressed. I still wasn't ready to face my demons.

Before I departed Göreme, I visited an engineering shop, where I got the broken seat springs welded. It was just as well: having seen Lynne off on her bus, I then bounced more than 20 kilometres along a rutted gravel road, a stretch that loosened all the rear spokes. I tightened the spokes, hoping they would hold. Thankfully, the surface improved, and — after only one steep hill, on which I had to push Effie more than 150 metres — life suddenly became easier.

Despite breaking several more spokes over the next couple of days, I covered 350 kilometres. Effie and I were in sync. But no sooner had I begun to relax than it all went pear-shaped, with the front wheel's bearings falling apart. This time I needed to get a front axle made. With several hundred kilometres still to go to Istanbul, all I could do was turn off to Gerede in search of an engineering shop.

Rock formations - Cappadocia, Turkey

A lonely & desolate region - Turkey

The shop owner, who didn't speak English, signalled that he would copy the original axle. I knew it was of a poor design, so I indicated I wanted him to follow my drawn instructions. Which he did, and, in less than two hours, presented me with an axle made from a blank piece of steel. Just a diagram and a few gestures had resulted in a perfect job from a capable and obliging engineer.

Back on the road, and having fitted my last set of bearings, the steering was much improved. But now I had no source of replacements. Two spares had been brought for the journey, and another two had been made in Pakistan. I reasoned that it was the bent axle that had caused the bearings to collapse, so, with a straight axle, I hoped there'd be no recurrence of the problem.

Now beyond Central Anatolia, I was riding on the gentle undulating D100 highway that meanders through a farming region. It was a comfortable, effortless ride. But conditions didn't stay that way for long, and, with strong headwinds, it was taking immense concentration to keep Effie on the right side of the road.

During this ordeal, I was stopped by two young men driving a van decorated with an image of one of their Repsol super bikes. These race riders were trying to tell me something, so they phoned a friend to translate.

The man on the phone said: 'They want to eat you.'

I hoped he meant: 'They want to invite you to lunch.'

The guys threw my backpack in the back of their van, instructed me to follow them, and took off. Doh! I'd just committed the cardinal sin of giving my gear to someone I didn't know. I might never see it again. Everything I had was in that backpack — including the carnet. If Lynne had been there, she would have had my guts for garters. Jeez, am I a slow learner!

But they were genuine, and directed me to their motorcycle shop, Inan Motors, where they put Effie into the showroom. There, a mechanic, who set about cleaning her, was in for a rude shock. As he turned the back wheel, the motor kicked into life. An incredulous look spread across the startled fellow's face. It was priceless, and everyone fell about laughing. We were still chuckling as we tucked into a tasty lunch of kebabs, rice, bread and the ubiquitous watermelon.

Adil, the owner, kindly gave me new cables and nipples as spares. What a great bunch they were. We all shook hands and said our goodbyes, and I set off towards Istanbul.

I was nearing Izmit, with just 100 kilometres still to go, and nightfall was approaching. After recent events, my smart choice would have been to look for a hotel. But I've never claimed to be smart, and hotels are never easy to find.

So I pulled onto the next level spot — the grassed roundabout entering the freeway — and set up my tent. No one seemed to mind me being there, and the police didn't ask me to move on. It was a little noisy and passing headlights shone through the tent, but I got a few hours' sleep.

At daylight, I was off again. As the city of Istanbul loomed up, I was gripped by an urge to flee. The freeway seemed to be going on forever, and I was glad I hadn't tried to find my way there in the dark. After a couple of hours, it seemed as though I was no closer. At one stage, heavy congestion, due to bridge repairs, forced me to walk the motorcycle along the hard shoulder. This was more effective than trying to cope with the stop-start early-morning traffic.

I spotted a Starbucks sign and went in for coffee and cake, and to wash and change into more presentable clothes. Given my diet of the past few months, the rich chocolate cake was almost too much, but the coffee gave me new life. I rode back into the chaos and worked my way towards Taksim Square, stopping occasionally to get my bearings.

As I peered at my map, I heard a voice yell, 'Mr Ron, Mr Ron.'

I looked around.

'Mr Ron, over here!'

A young man held out his hand and introduced himself as Mal. It turned out that this member of the Istanbul Bisiklet Motosiklet Ihtisas Kulubu had been following my blog and he'd been waiting a couple of weeks to meet me. I was staggered.

Mal though, thought nothing of it. He took me across the road to his office, made me coffee, introduced me to his workmates, and telephoned other club members. Then Effie and I followed him to Beyoglu, where Lynne had arranged a homestay.

For the next few days we took in all Istanbul had to offer: the Blue Mosque with its striking azure tiles and magnificent domed ceilings, the Grand Bazaar, the shops displaying mounds of mouthwatering sweets and the colourful ice cream vendors, and much more.

Before leaving Istanbul, I arranged to have a coffee with my erstwhile riding companion, Hayashi. It was good to hear all had gone well for him since we parted in Iran. He was heading for the Turkish coast, while I was on my way to Bulgaria.

The weather was becoming warmer, so I stripped down to a T-shirt, a pleasant change from my usual clobber. My feet weren't causing as much pain now I no longer had to use them to make those crazy, urgent stops, but the toenails were still a gruesome sight.

Surprisingly, Istanbul was relatively easy to get out of, and the border crossing is very organised — no delays, touts or pushy moneychangers. Best of all, the price of petrol halved once I was in Bulgaria, where I got much better value when exchanging dollars for levs. I intended to make the most of that advantage while it lasted.

Lynne was not so lucky...

28

Tree Pigs

Lynne ran into a long delay after crossing the border into Bulgaria. Her bus, bound for Sofia, was driven to a shed where passengers were ordered to disembark and sit with their luggage. Half-a-dozen customs agents searched the vehicle. It was obvious, she said, from the methodical way they worked, they had done this many times before. When they turned up several hidden packages, the head honcho barked a direction at the passengers and, reluctantly, they began moving away from the bus.

Having no idea about what was being said Lynne stayed where she was until a plump middle-aged woman in a bright headscarf whispered, 'Smugglers', and indicated that Lynne should leave her belongings and follow her to the benches where the other passengers had moved.

Systematically, each person's bags were searched. Out came stashes of cigarettes and other contraband. Several people were taken aside and questioned. Rather than confiscate the illicit items, and allow the bus to proceed, the officers escorted the suspects to a room for further interrogation.

They were not in a hurry, and everyone had to wait. By now, the driver was getting impatient that his vehicle was being held up. It was more than an hour before the bus was cleared and passengers were told to board. Over the next few miles, there was a good deal of fist waving and shouting among the passengers, none of which made sense to Lynne, who was tired and wanted only to reach her destination in Sofia.

In the meantime, I was on the road to the village of Nikolaevo in the Stara Zagora Province, south-central Bulgaria. I tried to buy a local phone card along the way, but to get one I had to provide copies of my passport and, because I had no fixed address, I had to have proof of my right to be in the country. I tried three times to get a card before I was successful.

Heading to Sofia - Bulgaria

Stork nest - Bulgaria

River crossing to Romania

Earlier, in Turkey, when our phones had been blocked, we'd traipsed from one Turksel office to another to find out why. Eventually, we were given the bizarre explanation that the government was censoring foreign phones in an effort to combat black-marketeering. That would have been fine, except that we'd just bought new cards and no one was willing to provide a refund. Finally, after we'd staged a one-hour sit-in, a Turksel manager relented and returned our money.

When we were planning our Asia-Europe itinerary we had come across The Tree Pigs Homestay in Nikolaevo. Intrigued by the name, Lynne made a booking for me there. On arriving in the village, I asked directions from a couple of giggling girls. Able only to speak a few words of English, one of them said, 'Your father lives down there,' pointing to white-walled farmhouse not far away. The Tree Pigs, by now renamed Tikaani Villa, was still owned by the person we had made the booking with. A genial and colourful fellow, Charles, a keen motorcyclist, welcomed me like an old friend into his home.

Given the favourable weather, I declined a comfortable room in the ancient restored farmhouse, choosing instead to set up my tent in small orchard. My host proved to be a great cook and his food was superb. With each delicious meal, which we shared under the grape vine-covered courtyard, came a 2.5-litre bottle of beer — standard fare in Bulgaria.

A great storyteller, Gypsy, as Charles, a Brit, is known, briefed me on the challenges expats face when buying property in Bulgaria. It sounded all too familiar, much like my experience in Indonesia, the main difference from us being that Gypsy was obviously happy in his adopted country.

Early next day, he took me on a walk. We climbed steadily for an hour-and-a-half, mostly through fog, crossing gentle creeks fed by natural springs. We passed a farming couple tending their crop, and saw flocks of goats and sheep grazing the scrub-covered hills. As we reached the summit, the sun was just cresting the horizon, revealing a panorama of the village below and the distant hills.

After breakfast, making good use of Gypsy's well-equipped shed, I adjusted the rear wheel by re-shimming the bearing and re-setting the crown wheel. An old olive-oil tin served as the new shim. I'd been able to reduce weight by jettisoning spare petrol containers no longer needed. Now I was only using a smaller emergency oil container. It was dawning on me that, by journey's end, I'd know exactly what I should have been carrying and what I hadn't needed.

I'd found a replacement set of tyre levers for the stolen ones but, because they were plastic, I wasn't looking forward to testing their efficacy on my tough new tyre. Still, beggars can't be choosers. I was still searching for a tyre inflator that would screw into the spark-plug hole, but no luck so far. Fingers crossed, I trusted I'd complete my journey without needing one.

All that remains of the Nikolaevo tobacco-growing region are derelict buildings and drying racks. Littering the ground beneath neglected plum trees was ripe red and yellow fruit which, I was told, made passable liquor. Fruit on ancient mulberry trees hanging over the roadways stained cars parked beneath them.

I spent two days wandering the village. Storks roosting precariously in untidy nests on the tops of power poles tickled my fancy. Locals believe the birds bring good luck, so they are not molested. As a bird fancier and nature lover, I had the thrill of seeing eagles and peregrine falcons, and of listening to a chorus of loud bullfrogs, the like of which I'd never heard before.

There is a great charm about Nikolaevo's patchwork stone and adobe walls, Spanish-styled tiled roofs, and donkey carts parked under the eaves. I could see why people are attracted to buying property and restoring ancient buildings in this part of Bulgaria. And I was reminded how easily we can fall for the romance of a place — until the reality sets in. Of course, if we never tried anything, how would we ever know?

Gypsy gave Effie a push, and we were off, me giving a big wave to my warm-hearted friend. People in villages I passed through were dressed in drab baggy trousers, worn shirts and dark headscarves or caps — all signs of hardworking peasant life. Everyone was friendly, and I only had to say 'Australia' to raise a smile and hear, 'Ah, kang-oo-roo'.

It was June 28 when I reached Plovdiv, Bulgaria's second-largest city. Gypsy had said it was a place I shouldn't miss. I easily found the hotel I had been told about, but, as had often been the way, its rates were out of my price range. The kind proprietor took me to cheaper accommodation at the Raisky Kat B&B and Hostel, which was within my budget. I thanked the man for guiding me there, and promised to return to his restaurant that night for dinner. The Raisky Kat, close to Plovdiv's old city, made it convenient for me over the next two days to explore both ancient and modern Plovdiv.

As well as lots of boarded-up buildings in the newer part of the city, there were many restorations, contemporary sculptures, fountains and shady parks, all of which give Plovdiv a sense of life. Street sweepers seemed to be swirling away everywhere.

Up the hill in the old city, contrasting architectural styles stood side by side. Meticulously restored, there are buildings influenced by Roman, Gothic, Art Deco, Turkish, Greek and Russian architecture; fairy-tale gingerbread houses, carved wooden facades, steep turrets, wooden shutters, iron grilles, latticed windows... Some exteriors are adorned with intricate scrolls, garlands and frescoes, painted in candy-floss pink, chocolate brown with cream trim or pomegranate. Along the shady avenues, olde-worlde street lamps added to the charm.

It was explained to me that, in times past, houses were taxed on their width at ground level. To cut their tax bills, some owners had cleverly designed buildings so that their width increased significantly the higher they rose, many ending up almost touching neighbouring structures, looking like they might topple at any minute!

Outside buildings of historical significance are plaques commemorating former owners and their trades, such as, 'Hypocrate's old pharmacy museum built in 1872'.

Down a narrow cobbled walkway, I came across a Roman amphitheatre with splendid multi-storied columns, and got goosebumps strolling through underground passages once trodden by the people of an ancient civilisation.

That evening, I went to the restaurant as promised, and I was not disappointed: tender squid, succulent pork fillet, followed by delicious homemade ice cream. What more could a man ask for! I'd be there again the next night.

After my huge meal, as I strolled around the new city area, I noticed a large crowd gathering. My interest piqued, I discovered a second amphitheatre in which a school choir was performing. The music drifted on the warm evening air, the performance winning enthusiastic applause. I enjoyed that opportunity to share in the spirit of Plovdiv.

While I was out exploring, the hostel owner's five-year-old grandson had been allowed to sit on the FN, maybe for a photo. It seems the boy had opened the throttle so wide the nipple had been pulled off the cable. His grandfather, who had managed to screw it back on, was honest enough to tell me, so that later, if I had a problem, I would know where the trouble might be. No major harm done, but I did wish people wouldn't tinker with the old girl. Every part of her is fragile, and often irreplaceable without having to start making a new part from scratch.

Sofia wasn't much farther, and I relished the easy run on smooth roads through fields of golden sunflowers. 'Watch out, the traffic is horrid in Sofia,' warned Adrian, a chap we'd been corresponding with via the blog, and who I had arranged to meet in a few days. I figured, given he lived part of the year in Bulgaria, he had a good idea of the conditions, so it was with some trepidation that I approached the national capital's city limits.

29

Where Time Stood Still

Adrian's dire warnings soon had me chuckling. Sofia's streets, despite the criss-crossing tramlines, were easy to navigate, and I found the Red B&B with no difficulty at all. He obviously had no idea about the encounters I'd survived in Asian metropolises since leaving Nepal.

I reached Sofia a day before schedule, Lynne being due to join me the next day. We planned to spend three relaxing days together.

Sofia's free walking tour, we decided, was the best way to take in the city. Lasting nearly three hours, it took us to many places we might have missed through simply not knowing of their existence. We saw excavated Roman ruins only recently discovered when the underground metro was being constructed. It was fascinating to walk on that smooth cobbled roadway beneath a modern thoroughfare, imagining what life must have been like in those ancient times.

Sofia has a neglected feel about it, but its citizens exude a vibrant energy that augurs well for a country still in the early stages of developing its democracy. Modern apartment buildings are gradually taking over from the socialist-era apartment blocks. Outdoor dining is popular, gelaterias abound and fashion boutiques and luxury goods stores are making an appearance.

At an antique market in a city park, battle helmets, bayonets, and other war memorabilia, including identity cards and documents could be bought for a princely sum, each telling a story. Old women hawked handmade lace, but there were few tourists and sales were slow.

We decided to go to Veliko Tarnovo, 220 kilometres east of Sofia. While Lynne took the bus, I relied on Effie. The temperature plummeted when I reached the mountains and the sun dipped behind trees. So far, I hadn't had to pedal or push — that would come later. I was 28 kilometres short of Veliko Tarnovo when I decided it was time I made camp.

A motorcyclist stopped to tell me he owned a camping ground 10 kilometres back. Because I was well set up, I decided to stay where I was. Just on dusk, he returned with friends. They all wanted to check out Effie. He owned a 500cc OHC Jawa, a rarity these days, behind which he towed a little one-wheel trailer. I was already in bed, but the guys wanted to hear Effie running. Because they were motorcyclists I gladly obliged, delighted to see their faces light up when her valves started chattering.

Next morning, I met Adrian as arranged and together we rode to meet his wife, Sue, at their lovely restored home. These British expats, although they already had two friends staying with them, insisted Lynne and I stay as well.

Many expats are drawn to this old hillside town, among them Dave, who we hired to give us a guided tour in his old London cab. Dave kindly made me a transfer, listing most of the countries along my route, to put on Effie's tank. It was encouraging to realise I had already visited most of them.

We enjoyed hanging out with fellow bike enthusiasts, chatting over dinner, and indulging in cheap Bulgarian beer, which I have to admit, was pretty damn good.

This break from the rigours of my journey gave me a chance to remove the FN's barrels and inspect the pistons. I was apprehensive of what I might find. But all I needed to do was to remove a small amount of carbon build-up. I also gave the exhaust valves a quick lapping, even though that wasn't really necessary. I tried to buy a Bosch spark plug in Veliko Tarnovo to replace the one the porcelain had loosened on, but none was available. Nor could I find another brand suited to the required heat range.

I removed the sponge and vinyl from the seat that I'd put on in India, because it had now become compressed and uncomfortable. Adrian kindly gave me a bicycle gel seat cover to go under the seat's leather. It felt more flexible, and I would learn over the next few days how well it worked.

The pedalling chain had stretched, so I removed one link to tighten it. And, to make the dovetail tighter on the adjuster for the pedalling chain, I inserted a sliver of aluminium from a coke can. It worked well.

Rear spokes were still a problem. I had been replacing one or two every few days. I thought this was because the flange on the hub that the spoke went through was too thin and causing the spoke heads to be cut off. Unfortunately, I couldn't do anything about this because it meant dismantling the rear hub and finding an engineering shop to repair it. I figured I had enough spokes to see me to the end.

In a tiny antique shop, we came across old goggles, horns, gas lamps and other paraphernalia. Although not sure how authentic they were — I didn't really care — I bought a quaint pair of goggles with boggle-eyed glass.

In Sue and Adrian's lovingly restored 200-year-old house, it was soothing to wake to the sound of the chiming clock in the nearby square, and take in the spectacular second-storey view of the town.

Slowly, the challenges of recent weeks receded from my mind and I could feel my energy return. I was sure the worst was now behind me and as long as I could keep Effie going I could complete my journey.

Adrian was planning to leave for the Dracula rally in Romania in a few days' time — he could cover much greater distances on his bike than I could on mine — so we arranged to meet after I had crossed into Romania and ride together for a couple of days.

Before I left VT, as Veliko Tarnovo is known locally, we practiced erecting Adrian's odd shaped tent. He had lost the instructions, so it was the blind leading the blind. After a few attempts, we could only hope we had it right. I knew my little tent wasn't big enough for both of us.

Soon it was time for us to go our separate ways. I said my farewells, grateful especially to Sue for her wonderful hospitality. She was going back with her guests to Britain, and Lynne was booked on the bus to Bucharest.

Adrian stayed with me halfway to the Romanian border, and twice we got lost relying on his navigational skills. I was wondering if he knew any more than I did about Bulgarian roads. The remainder of the day was uneventful and I camped late afternoon in an industrial yard, after being told no ferries crossed the river into Romania until the next day.

I left my campsite early next morning, stopping for a coffee and a hot meat pastry along the way to the border ferry at Svishtov. I'd estimated I had plenty of time before it departed, but when I got there I learned there were only two boats a day, and one was leaving in a few minutes. It was a mad scramble to get the customs and immigration paperwork stamped and to buy a ticket before I was allowed to push Effie aboard and squeeze her in-between large trucks to the bow of the ferry. By 8.00 am, I was in Romania and about to go through the whole border fun and games again. It took three people to push and drag Effie up the steep ramp to the customs shed, where the formalities were pleasantly routine, but only after waiting for all the trucks to be processed.

A few kilometres short of Alexandria, a motorcyclist pulled alongside and introduced himself: 'Hi, I'm Costi. Welcome to Romania.' He said he'd been to Svishtov the previous day and had left his phone number with the authorities to hand to me on my arrival. As I hadn't arrived, he'd come looking for me again. I was amazed at how many people were showing interest in Effie and me; and how they would just pop up here and there and offer support in any way they could.

Costi, after reading about Effie on the blog, had taken a week off work to hook up with me. He lived in Bucharest, the Romanian capital, 88 kilometres from Alexandria, where his parents lived, and where Costi, his friend Andrei and I were now headed.

Along the way, we rode through Buzescu, home to a population of 5000 Romani people. Although nomads by tradition, many have given up their horse-drawn caravans. Some, largely financed by the Romani diaspora, now have multi-storey mansions complete with ornate turrets, columns, marble staircases, chandeliers and wide balconies. Many more Romani, however, are still in abject poverty and heavily dependent on remittances from family members working around Europe.

The Romani, renowned metal traders, for many generations made copper stills (cazane) that sold at high prices. But taxes and regulations governing homemade liquor limit production to a handful today. In 1989, when communist-run countries were rapidly imploding, enterprising Romani began accumulating wealth by selling metal scavenged from shuttered factories.

Romani, not without reason, tend to be suspicious of outsiders, and do not encourage visitors to take photos. As we passed through the streets of Buzescu, I was amazed at how ostentatious the houses were. I also noticed many manhole covers were missing. Given that each weighed more than 130 kilograms they certainly wouldn't have been easy to remove.

I spent that night with Costi and his parents, his mum serving a delicious traditional meal of sarmale and polenta. Next morning, Andrei joined us on a ride towards Pitesti because he works in a factory along the way. After Andrei left us, I lost sight of Costi behind me so I stopped to wait for him. He eventually turned up in a very sorry state. What had happened was that, with the road surface rough, he had taken a heavy fall on a sandy corner. We managed to straighten out the headlight and blinkers and, with five-minute Araldite from my toolkit, I glued the headlight brackets together. Costi bought plasters from a nearby store for the scrapes on his arms and knees. Although shaken, and feeling pretty sore, he was more worried about what his parents would say on seeing his damaged bike.

We spent the next few hours wandering around Pitesti's town square, enjoying lunch and exchanging dollars for local currency, new lei (singular leu). Before parting, Costi introduced me to his friend Mike, at whose house I was to spend the night. While in Pitesti, the guys at National Car Company Dacia welded 40 spokes for me, and, like so many other wonderfully generous people along the way, they refused payment. I hoped Costi had made it home in one piece. I was very grateful to this generous young man for all the kindness he had shown me.

Because he lived in an apartment, and there was no room for Effie, Mike suggested he take a taxi and I follow him to the secure parking area at his workplace. That evening, we walked to a restaurant for dinner and a couple of beers. Next morning, we caught a bus to his workplace to collect Effie, and I left town, riding north to Curtea de Arges.

Romania was very much how I had envisaged it. The countryside is green and rambling, cottages have neatly tended vegetable gardens, and horses and carts are in common use. The senses tell you that this is a place where time is standing still. As I rode into Curtea de Arges, I spied a couple of Triumph motorcycles outside a restaurant. I was making a u-turn when one of the Triumph riders came running out. 'Wow, I thought I saw a four-cylinder,' he exclaimed. The two British bikers swapped travel tales with me before we wished each other, 'Safe journey'.

I wanted to explore, so I asked a market stallholder to keep an eye on Effie. I wandered into the grounds of the Curtea de Arges monastery, whose early-16th-century stone cathedral featured spiralled Moorish cupolas and narrow-slit windows. This sculptured building, dedicated to Saint Nicholas, is adorned with intricate mouldings and arabesques. The effect is of a giant wedding cake.

On my return to the bike, the stallholder proudly attached a miniature Romanian flag to the handlebars and, with a broad smile, waved me off. I asked the police at a nearby police station if I could camp in the city park. 'No, it's dangerous,' they said, and offered to lead me to a camping ground at the nearby village of Noaptes. The place had fantastic amenities specifically for motorcyclists, and, along with neat little chalets, it had the best hot showers. Breakfast, dinner and beers were also available. Vali, the owner, kindly offered me the use of his extensive workshop where he services KTMs that are rented out to off-road enthusiasts. That's where I adjusted the spokes in readiness for the next day's challenge.

I returned to Curtea de Arges by bus next morning, keen to explore the rest of the town while waiting for Adrian to arrive in the afternoon. The plan was that we would ride together the rest of the way to Turda via the Fagarashan Mountains, where the road rises to 2,544 metres. We planned to camp along the way, but unfortunately Adrian arrived minus his tent, having failed to secure it properly on the back of his 500cc Gilera. 'I think I felt it come off,' he said nonchalantly, 'but I didn't stop to check.'

Directly after breakfast, we set off for Curtea de Arges. The gel seat Adrian had given me was working a treat. It was good to be riding in comfort at last. The road twisted and turned as it wound its way higher and, in the crisp morning air, my breath started to come in puffy little clouds. Despite a few rough spots, the conditions weren't nearly as bad as I'd been led to believe. But boy, was that road steep!

Adrian kindly did the honours by push-starting the bike each time she overheated or ran out of breath — in all, about 20 times. Finally, he wised up and flagged down other motorcyclists, encouraging them to share his load.

The views at the top of the pass were stupendous. Mountain peaks, some still with traces of snow, and switchbacks all the way down the other side. It was some of the most spectacular scenery I'd seen since leaving Nepal.

Because of the sand scuffed to the middle of each corner, the hairpin bends were extra tricky for a long-wheel-based motorcycle like the FN. It was fortunate that I'd been warned of those particularly dangerous spots.

It turned into a long day. Adrian rode on into Sibiu, leaving me to continue at my own pace. Soon after he disappeared from sight, two policemen stepped out onto the roadway and flagged me down. This looked ominous. One, peering at the machine, asked: 'Why is your headlight not going?'

'It's hard to find carbide in Romania,' I quipped.

I don't know if he understood, but the fact I was being asked made me decide, there and then, to switch over to the LED light in the lamp to save further hassles. 'Do you need a license to ride that thing?'

I foolishly answered, 'Yes', so of course they wanted to see it. We went through the usual checks. They inspected the bike; they read through all the documentation; they asked me where I'd been and where I was going;

and they took note of my blog address. Eventually, I was cleared and they gave me a push start. I was on my way again.

I finally found Adrian in a rather expensive place — he's not one for camping in drains — and, because I was beat, I joined him in what was a superb hotel. We had been lucky to get a room because it was almost booked out by competitors in a car rally. After a restful night's sleep, we enjoyed a great buffet breakfast that stood us in good stead for the rest of the day.

With Adrian still riding on ahead, I decided to deviate from my route plan and travel on back roads via Sugag. My main aim was to avoid the freeway. I had only travelled a short distance when the clip on the inlet valve spring broke. This I fixed with a small piece cut off a spare exhaust-valve spring. The route change I had made would give me an opportunity to compare restored and unrestored villages. It would also result in one of the rides of my life.

House of the People - Bucharest, Romania

Fargaras Mountain Road - Romania

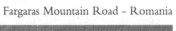

30

Evel Knievel

On my way to Sugag, after one long hard climb which got tougher as it went, I suddenly found myself over the top and hurtling down the steepest road I'd ever had the misfortune to encounter. Brakes full on, engine killed, yet Effie was still doing her minimum speed of 19 kmh — and I had no hope of stopping her.

I hung on, knuckles whitening as we slalomed. Thinking it couldn't get worse, I skidded around a sharp bend and was horrified to see an excavator clearing a rockslide spread across the road. Escape? Over the edge of the cliff, infinity! On the road, a tiny gap, but only as long as the excavator didn't fill it! Could I squeeze through? For a second, I wanted to pray (but to which gods should I turn?). Was unseen traffic coming up the hill I was careering down? Would I slam into the loader? Whichever course I took, I felt I was a goner.

Effie, her little valves clattering, tore into the stretch of roadworks. No traffic controllers in sight, but suddenly workmen gesturing and shouting. No chance to wave back — and photo opportunities were definitely out!

I swerved past the excavator, flashing within inches of parked vehicles. Effie, in her element, was refusing to slow. And I couldn't think about throwing myself off because my bum was glued to the seat. In the distance, a T-junction, and just before it the descent began to level out. I let the decompressor go, turned on the fuel and closed the air lever. Effie fired instantly, her momentum reducing just enough to allow the brakes to take effect. We lurched to a halt, I stumbled off and sank to my knees, heart pounding. Effie, who was having had the ride of her life, stood innocently by.

A motorist, approaching from the junction, stopped and came across the road. 'Are you alright?'

I took my head out of my hands, looked up, and nodded. 'What's the road like to Sibiu?' he asked. 'It's a breeze,' I assured him.

It was a while before I recovered sufficiently to climb back on, and immediately decided I would have to call it a day. That crazy ride had been a heart-stopper, and I knew I wasn't up to making the rendezvous I had planned with Adrian.

At the next town of Sugag, I stopped to eat, and when I asked about accommodation the old lady offered me a room. I was just settling in when Adrian phoned. 'I'm not going any further today, mate,' I told him. 'It's been a tough day. I've got a great place here to stop for the night.'

'Well, the one I found is a dump,' he said. 'So I'll come and join you.'

Our host served a delicious home-style meal, and plenty of it, and we washed it down with traditional plum spirits. I slept like a baby, waking to yet another bright sunny day. After nearly six months on the road, I had encountered rain only once while I was riding — in Nepal. Either I'd been bloody lucky, or we really had planned my journey well.

Adrian rode on ahead when we set off for Turda. I was happy to travel at a slower pace, stopping when I felt the need. On a coffee break at the Benstar fuel station, the owner, Crisan, generously offered me free petrol. I'd filled up a little earlier, but gratefully accepted two litres for my spare container. Continuing on to Turda, I made a short detour to the Dumbrava Judtul-Alba monastery, and wandered around its expansive grounds and well-kept gardens.

When I sat down for a rest in the shade, a young man, in halting English, asked, 'Are you alright?'

'Yes, I'm just resting,' I said.

'Wait please,' he said, and hurried off. A few minutes later, he was back with a young nun, who asked, 'Would you like to stay for lunch?' I accepted, and followed her to the upstairs kitchen and dining area. She explained that the monastery cared for 87 orphans and 40 elderly people. Asked why she had chosen such a vocation, she replied, with a smile, 'I've had a previous life'.

Huge mounds of roast chicken, vegetables, fresh bread and homemade chocolate biscuits were set before me. At the nun's insistence, I ate until I could swallow no more. When I offered to pay, she shook my hand and wished me well. 'Thank you, but that's not necessary. You are our guest.' Yet again, I was overwhelmed by the generosity of so many that I was meeting along my way.

The ride on into Turda was uneventful, and we arrived a couple of days before the city's annual Dracula Rally. Lynne arrived the next day from Veliko Tarnovo, via Bucharest, the capital of Romania, a country still shrugging off its communist era. Over dinner, I asked her what she thought of Bucharest.

'Parts of the city had the appearance of a shabby overcoat,' she said. 'Dilapidated apartments were covered with graffiti. The place I stayed in was grotty, with rickety stairs and poor lighting. It turned out to be the worst homestay I've ever been in. It was only when I went for a Sunday morning walk that I discovered another side to the city.'

Lynne found graffiti being removed and buildings being freshly painted, in an effort to brighten up the city. Here, restaurant patrons, sipping beers and enjoying their meals, sat outside under striped umbrellas.

In the city's historical district, Lynne said, 30,000 homes and at least 30 churches and synagogues had been razed in 1980 to make way for a huge structure comprising Nicolai Ceausescu's residence and the parliament buildings he would dominate. With 1,100 rooms, this immense edifice, ironically named the People's House, was never completed. The parking area was jammed with tour buses, and people waited in queues to ogle one of Ceausescu's most extreme examples of shameless self-indulgence.

Lynne had been subject to attempted extortion by a taxi driver who had delivered her to her Bucharest hotel. Not one to meekly accept being ripped off, she called on hotel management to confront the cheating cabbie, who had quadrupled his fare. Only when staff threatened to call the police did he grudgingly accept the correct amount, tossing Lynne's bags on the roadway and hurling abuse at her before speeding away.

Despite there being several of the city's most impoverished citizens camped around the Gara de Nord railway station, the general crime rate in Bucharest was said to be low when compared with other European capitals; and unemployment was claimed to be an impressive 2.1 per cent.

It was from the Gara de Nord that Lynne took a train to Sighisoara, a mediaeval town in the historic northern region of Transylvania. She said it lived up to its reputation as one of the most picturesque villages in Romania, but the hordes of tourists packing the cobbled streets definitely didn't sound like my cup of tea.

On her departure from Sighisoara, intending to go to Turda, Lynne was unable to find anyone on the station who spoke English and took a punt on which train to catch — and, of course, she picked the wrong one. Her error was discovered when the conductor came through to check her ticket. In a panic, Lynne, with all her baggage, clambered off at the next station — and waited for a train that would take her all the way to Turda.

The Hunter Prince Castle & Dracula hotel, where we were staying for the next few days, had the idiosyncrasies, inside and out, of an eccentric hunting lodge. Despite the quirky decor, the rooms are comfortable and our meals were delicious. Among wild boar, venison, bear and quail on the menu, we gave Tired Dracula's Dick, a pork meatloaf with mushrooms, a miss.

In the evening, over chilled beer, we chatted with Mike and Tim, motorcyclists who had ridden to Romania from Britain. Like us, they had expectations that the annual Dracula rally was going to be huge event. However, with so few foreign riders turning up, it didn't look as if it was going to be quite the affair we'd been hoping for.

The Transylvania Riders Motorcycle Club's main objective for the weekend had been to recreate the road race the club first held there in the 1947 — a time trial over one kilometre. Most participants were local riders on mainly 1960s' bikes and war-issue bikes with sidecars, some with mounted machine guns. The last official race through the streets of Turda was in 2009 and, with opposition to street racing having grown so much, this year there would only be a parade of bikes followed by a sprint time trial.

Nevertheless, the rally did provide the opportunity for us to meet some wonderfully generous and hospitable people. Effie took part in the time trial and, though she didn't actually burn rubber, she didn't let the side down, starting first go and achieving a respectable time. I got an 'old-bloke' award for distance travelled and a bottle of champagne to commemorate the event.

Tim and Mike, who were heading back to Britain via a scenic route, in a kind gesture of motorcycling solidarity, made a donation towards my expenses.

Over the next week, Lynne and I toured northeastern and western Romania in a rental car. It made a pleasant change to be in a comfortable vehicle, and I'm sure Effie appreciated the rest.

Romania abounds with stunningly beautiful, unspoiled countryside. Our route, through mountain and valleys, took us to quaint villages of ornately decorated houses and barns, their fancy gables, carvings and tin ornamentation kept our cameras clicking. Much of the architecture has World Heritage status. There are dense forests, and alpine meadows where cheerful rotund women harvest hay with long pitchforks. Horses pull open wooden carts loaded with scrap iron. And, here and there, Romani women in sequined long skirts and brightly coloured scarves sell freshly picked berries.

So many churches and monasteries in Romania are adorned inside and out with colourful frescos. Intriguing graveyards took up a lot of our interest, especially the richly decorated Merry, cemetery of Sapanta in the Maramures region close to the border with Ukraine. There, wooden grave markers are painted with scenes depicting the dead.

In 1935, Stan Patras, a Sapanta artist, began carving and painting tombstones with often-amusing tales about the lives of the dead, or about events relevant to their lives. Over the next 50 years, more than 800 tombstones were so adorned. They attract thousands of visitors. Maramures, because of the architecture of its wooden houses and barns, and its mode of transport, is as near-to-mediaeval as anywhere in Europe. But, as in all tourist settlements, there are the usual stalls selling everything from gnomes to fake fur hats and toffee apples!

I've been an apiarist since my teenage years, so I was fascinated to see scores of brightly painted mobile hive transporters in fields. It's an amazing way not only to move bees from one location to another, but to keep them warm through winter months. With meadows ablaze with flowers, I could only imagine the activity going on inside all those hives.

Eastern Europe is renowned for its castles, and against a stunning backdrop of the Carpathian Mountains Peles Castle did not disappoint.

With Effie resting in Turda, the deviation from my schedule enabled me to see a good deal more of Romania than I might otherwise have done. I know that with time, the little FN could have tackled the steep switchback roads, but it didn't make sense to add more miles than necessary to the bike's journey. She had already proven her worth and we still had some distance to go before the end.

While in Romania, I got an email from the Guinness Book of Records saying they thought my ride wouldn't 'create enough public interest', and that it 'was a little too specialised for a body of reference as general' as theirs.

I guess it's hard to pit one's claim against someone who has stuffed his face with the 'biggest falafel', or against the 'most people in one bed together'! It would have been nice if my unique achievement were recognised by that well-known publication, but, from the interest shown, I know there were plenty who were following what Effie and I were doing.

Oncoming traffic - Romania

Lining up for the start - Turda, Romania

Turda Time trial - Romania

31

Taking it Slow

Back in Turda, we went to where we had left Effie, with Alin, the motorcycle-rally organiser. I felt my life was getting too 'cruisey', and wanted to get back in the saddle. Soon I headed off, under heavy skies and wearing rain-gear. I left Lynne waiting for an overnight lift to Budapest with Alin's friend who, with his partner, drives a van to Italy to pick up secondhand motorcycles for resale in Romania.

I covered only 100 kilometres before deciding to call it a day, and camped at an abandoned gas station just off the freeway. I was well asleep when, sometime after midnight, headlights shining through the tent woke me. I staggered out to find the two guys Lynne was hitching a ride with, had stopped to take a close look at Effie. Bleary eyed, I shook hands with them, waited while they gave her the once-over, then crawled back into my sleeping bag.

Having achieved so little the previous day, I was keen to make up time. Also, I was hoping for an easy border crossing into Hungary. With Romania behind me, I got to thinking about Adrian and Laura, the couple I met in Iran. They provided me with so much useful information and suggestions about what to see and do in Romania. Thanks to them, Lynne and I had been able to take a really good look at a fabulous country, one I'd very much like to revisit.

At the crossing, the Hungarian customs officials welcomed me with coffee, and then sent me on my way with a bottle of water. Same as for Romania, only my passport needed stamping. Now that I was in the European Union, I no longer had to present the carnet for the bike. Little did I know this would cause me hassles down the track. I easily found a phone card, but not all of my first day in the EU was to go as planned.

The back roads I chose were rough. As a result, another six spokes broke and, yet again, Effie's power began to ebb away. That night was largely sleepless as I tried to figure out what to do about her. Life was tough enough without having endless mechanical problems to solve. Sharing my frustrations with Lynne during our evening phone sessions helped me to get problems off the chest and into some sort of perspective. Most answers were usually with me by morning.

At first light, I checked the magneto and found the carbon brush had seized and burnt down. This meant it was not possible for the spring to be pushed far enough down. I set about trying to free up the brush, and finally managed a repair of sorts. I could only hope I'd solved the problem.

Formal campsites were hard to find at the end of each day, and usually I was knackered, so I camped where I could. When I was about to set up my tent in the carpark of the TTL Carpet shop at Miskolo, I joked about being 'used to the hard ground', but then gratefully accepted the owner's generous offer of carpet pieces to soften the tent floor.

Earlier in the day, at a supermarket, I bought a roll, ham, tomatoes, cheese and a bottle of milk that would last me two days. That evening, I dined on a can of rice-filled-cabbage rolls. I'd eaten well during the past week and now I was back to rations.

On the way next day, I was alarmed by a banging noise coming from the engine. I was getting jumpy: would Effie's engine make it to Belgium before dying completely? The little bike had already exceeded expectations, and I felt I owed it to her to do all I could to help her see the journey through.

On my way across the Great Plain, which covers much of eastern and southern Hungary, I stopped at the Barna windmill in Karcag. There, Gabor, the caretaker, spent a couple of hours showing me around and explaining the workings of the largest windmill in Eastern Europe. It had operated from 1859 to 1949. The mill's centre post is a whopping two-foot-square oak beam, and the big gear is willow, with acacia for the teeth. With each grinding stone weighing 500 kilos, the mill could process 200 kilos of flour in an hour. The sail had to turn only once for the stone to turn 35 times.

I made it to Szolnok, where I had booked my first night's paid accommodation in Hungary. The engine noise problem had been nagging me all day, so I checked Effie all over. I noticed, as I attempted to undo the spark plug terminal, that the porcelain on the steel body of the spark plug had come loose. This was allowing air to be sucked in and a small amount of compression to be blown out. But none of this was happening until the plug had heated up. By replacing the Bosch plugs with NGKs the frightening noise went away. However, compared with the plugs I had started out with, no replacement was quite as efficient.

I tried to avoid freeways whenever possible, even though at times they were preferable because of the helpful signage. The downside of freeway travel was that I attracted the attention of the police. 'You're going too slow,' complained one officer. 'The minimum speed on the highway is 60 kmh,' said his partner.

The FN's handbook emphasised that Effie was capable of 100 kmh because of its high gearing. However, with beaded edge tyres it was more reassuring sitting at a much lower speed. Because I preferred to travel at less than 60 kmh, I carried a bogus document saying my bike was only capable of only 40 kmh. I'd met no minimum speed limits earlier in my travels, so it usually made sense to produce it when police insisted I travel faster. But now the tables were turned: no good me claiming the bike could only do 40 kmh, so I agreed to turn off at the next exit.

I waited in a rest area and enjoyed a coffee with local riders. Trying to find my way into any city via back roads is always an ordeal, so I debated with myself about defying the law and hopping back onto the freeway. I was aware that the police, though they had been sympathetic to my dilemma, might not be quite so accommodating if they saw me a second time. Nevertheless, I decided to risk it. When I figured enough time had passed, I went back on the freeway and headed for Budapest, the Hungarian capital. I got away with it.

Budapest is a maze of tramlines that run like trenches in the road. They grabbed at Effie's skinny tyres as I worked my way towards the Lord Apartments, our accommodation for the next few days. At each red light, I had to turn off the motor, and then push-start Effie as soon as the lights changed. This involved frantically running alongside the bike and clambering on when she fired, all the while fighting to balance my heavy backpack. By the time I arrived at our apartment, my legs had turned to jelly, my head hurt and Effie was boiling. I was ready for a stiff drink after yet another capital city baptism of fire!

As if in answer to my prayers, I was almost instantly invited to share in a celebratory drink by a just-married bridegroom who had rushed across the road from a small crowd gathered outside a reception centre. By my second slug of palinka, a traditional Hungarian fruit brandy, I was ready to tackle anything!

Lynne's journey hadn't been all beer and skittles, either. On the day I left Turda, it was 11.00 pm before the guys she'd hitched a ride with arrived to pick her up. She said the men, accustomed to long night hauls, had no problem with sleeping in shifts, while the other travelled at high speed in a mist of road spray, between heavy vehicles.

Unable to stretch out, she was stiff and exhausted by the time the van pulled into a truck stop on the outskirts of Budapest. She thanked her companions, and staggered into a motel to call a taxi. She'd had no sleep for more than 24 hours and it would be another two hours before she got to the Lord Apartments. It was, she said, like jetlag but without the frequent-flyer points.

Seeing drooping shoulders and dark rings around Lynne's eyes, the receptionist said, 'Oh you poor dear, you look exhausted. Here, take a seat and rest while I get you a cup of tea and we prepare your room.' Before Lynne could say thanks, she was racing for the lavatory. It was yesterday's curry's revenge. Fortunately, by the time I arrived, the stomach bug had been controlled by a strong dose of Flagyl, and she recovered sufficiently to join me for a late lunch. We mused on the fact that Lynne had mostly eaten in restaurants yet had become ill twice, whereas I had eaten practically anywhere and got away with it.

As usual, once we'd unpacked, showered and caught up with the laundry, we spent hours writing up the blog and planning the next stages. I contacted Andras, a Hungarian I had met in Sofia a few weeks earlier, and arranged for us to meet again.

He took us under his wing, arriving at dusk to give us a tour of his beautiful city, pointing out examples of architecture we might have missed on our own. I shivered when he described how tanks had rolled through the streets during the Soviet Moscow's invasion of Hungary in 1956. It was hard to imagine what that must have felt like for the inhabitants.

Andras arranged for us to visit the Transport Museum and to attend a press conference. I was overwhelmed by the huge turnout of motorcyclists, staff, public and media as I entered City Park and then the museum entrance. With Andras translating, I talked about my journey. Then, I was presented with a 'certificate of achievement', and a commemorative medallion by Janos, the museum's organiser.

I was humbled by this recognition of something that, after all, was simply a fulfilment of a dream. But I also was aware that what I was doing had never been done before. Few could imagine the trials I'd been through to get that far. And that clanging noise that Effie had been making was telling me just how fragile the little bike was.

After interviews and photographs, Lynne and I were treated to lunch and a tour of the museum, an impressive collection of historic motorcycles, cars, trains and maritime transports.

During my final few days in Budapest, I agreed to be interviewed by Andras for a magazine interested in my travels. I'd been interviewed many times, and found it easy to share my story. I did my best to always put a positive spin on my experiences of travelling across a world that many consider dangerous. This time though, I came unstuck.

32

Spilling the Beans

'Count me out, this isn't about me,' said Lynne, over breakfast, when Andras asked her a question. 'But I want to hear your story too,' he urged. 'In the short time I've known you both, I can see that you are a real team.' Andras continued to draw on our experiences, gently probing to build his picture.

'Did you ever find yourself in any real danger?'

'Well, I was robbed once in Iran,' I admitted. 'And a gun was held to my head in Turkey.'

Lynne's jaw dropped. 'What!'

I'd forgotten I hadn't shared the gun episode with her, and instantly I wanted to take it all back, so shaken was she.

'Why didn't you tell me?' she challenged, her face whitening.

Andras averted his eyes, clearly uncomfortable to be witnessing the scene.

'I didn't want to worry you, and it shook me up so much I had to put it out of my mind if I was going to continue,' I confessed.

'Tell me what happened? Was it on the way from Dogubayazit?'

'Yes, the day after we talked about the region being risky.'

So at last, I found myself telling the story, leaving nothing out.

Lynne took my hand. 'I wish I'd known, so I could have been there for you.' She was holding back tears, trying to get her head around how different things might have been had the teenager pulled the trigger.

Andras, who had sat quietly listening, asked, 'Do you want me to include this in the article?'

We discussed the pros and cons, and agreed that it would colour the impression others had of the very people I had found so uplifting. It wasn't that I wanted to paint the world as all hearts and flowers. That

Budapest - Hungary

Starting demonstration, Tech Museum, Budapest - Hungary

would be naive. But the vast majority of people I had met were generous and kind, and quite unlike how they are often portrayed in the media.

Rather than have others being fearful of living their dreams, I wanted to inspire them; to demonstrate that we can seek adventure at any age, and to show them living life to the full can sometimes involve taking risks. At the same time, I wanted to emphasise that, most of the time, people are just like Lynne and me; they live their everyday lives, wanting only to have a home, a job, food on the table and education for their kids.

Yes, there are bullies and thieves, but they are just as often found in boardrooms, offices and in schools as on the highways of Iran and the back roads of Turkey. The feedback I was getting daily was demonstrating to me just how many people's views had been changed as a result of reading our blog. Yes, we decided, there would be a time for telling all — but that time was not now.

We continued with the interview, Andras extracting from me many aspects of my travels that I had forgotten. When it was over, Lynne and I hugged Andras goodbye. It was time to explore more of the city.

Perhaps it's the architecture, the wide avenues, the eternal signs and an all-pervasive sense of history — there's something about European cities that is especially captivating for travellers from the other side of the world.

By now, the temperature was soaring. Despite being 40 degrees Celsius, the City of Bridges had us in its spell. A real eye-catcher is the castle on the Buda (western) side of the Danube. At that point, the Danube is crossed by the Chain Bridge, a suspension structure built in 1849, and the first permanent linking of Buda and Pest.

I'd really enjoyed Hungary and felt a need to return some day, especially to catch up with Andras. Lynne had been considering a river cruise to Germany, but decided she'd probably be bored after only one day on a boat, let alone several, so she opted to take the train to Vienna after staying a few days longer in Budapest. Meanwhile, I would be riding through Slovakia to Austria. When we said goodbye in Budapest, it was, not surprisingly, with a little more feeling than on previous partings.

Crossing borders with no questions being asked was taking a little getting used to. The road between Sahy and the spa town of Dudince, in southern Slovakia, runs through gently rolling hills, so it was an easy ride before I made camp. I found that I was relishing the shorter European stages after all those long hauls across Asia.

A boy of about 10 stopped his cycle to watch me servicing Effie. He stayed nearly three hours, all the time trying his best to make conversation. He was totally absorbed in all I was doing, and was tickled pink when I gave him a Bounty bar. Later that evening, an older youth walked me across a steel bridge that the Germans had shelled during World War II, then presented me with a large Slovakian flag. The gesture was appreciated, but goodness knows how I was going to carry it.

All next day, Effie backfired. The NGK plugs had not lasted well. I knew when the trip was over, that I would need to strip her down to do some serious work. I had been considering riding her back home again, but I knew now she probably wouldn't be up to it without a complete engine overhaul.

I was camped in a park just beyond Galanta, enjoying a dinner of fresh bread rolls full of cheese and tomato, when a Slovakian motorcyclist and his girlfriend stopped by. I asked them the word for spark plug. Next morning, I went back to Galanta and asked a police officer where I could buy new plugs. He didn't fully understand what I was saying, so he escorted me to the city hall, where an interpreter asked a police driver to go and buy new plugs for me. The ones he got were not what I would have liked, but they did the job, and I was extremely grateful. Viliam, the police officer insisted on buying me a chicken roll for breakfast. By that time, a crowd had gathered, so I got a rousing farewell.

Later in the day, near Bratislava, I was stopped by a sleek black chauffeured SUV. The passenger got out and shook my hand. 'I've been following your blog and would like to be a minor sponsor,' said Peter, pressing paper currency into my hand. That generous donation, which was the biggest I'd received since starting my journey, was warmly appreciated.

We posed together for a few photos and, again, a group gathered. I gained the impression that Peter was a well-known identity. Among the crowd was a vintage-car enthusiast, someone I thought would appreciate the flag I'd been given. Judging by the smile on his face, I was right.

I had always imagined the final stages of my journey would be easier, and, in many respects, they were. However, a big difference was that now, cities and towns were so much closer. As always, each time one came in sight, I approached with trepidation — urban areas always tax my nerves. But in Europe I was sensing something different: there was none of the chaos of India, or the bone-shaking roads of Pakistan; and there was none of the nervous excitement in crowds that threatened to overwhelm me when I was in Asia. The mental and physical challenges of negotiating traffic were similar, regardless of the environment, but the cultural differences in Europe were so much easier to handle. The truth was that I missed the adrenalin rush, the colours, the smells and the intensity of India, Pakistan and Iran.

I crossed the border into Austria without even noticing and rode on into Vienna on a miserably cold and wet day. On the city outskirts, I rode down an off-ramp and under the freeway, only to find it wasn't leading in the direction I wanted to go. I turned around and pushed Effie back up the ramp against the oncoming traffic. While I was catching my breath at the top of the ramp, a motorist stopped and offered to show me the way. I followed him for a few kilometres to his house, where I waited while he ran inside with groceries for his wife. At the next junction he instructed me to ride through six intersections, then take a left turn.

But Effie was having none of it. Sheeting rain filled my boots, and I shivered as I pushed her through one intersection after another. The distributor soon became waterlogged, forcing me to repeatedly stop and mop it out with a rag. It was perilous trying to keep the bike on an even keel over slippery surfaces, especially when crossing the many tramlines.

My three shirts, a jacket and wet-weather gear clung to my skinny frame, and my teeth chattered. In six hours, I had only covered 120 kilometres and I was desperate to be somewhere dry and warm. Once again I had somehow missed the turn, and when I stopped to ask directions from the police, they wanted to check my papers.

I was hungry, too. I sloshed my way into a takeaway and woofed down a kebab. I knew I was very near the homestay we had booked, but I couldn't wait to eat. The owner, taking pity on me, handed me another kebab. No charge. I promised to return on a sunny day so that he could take a photo of Effie standing outside his shop. That was only the second time I had been caught in heavy rain, and I didn't enjoy the discomfort. At last I reached my accommodation, where a hot bath brought me back to life. Soon, snug and warm, I was sleeping like a baby.

Next day, under emerald skies, Lynne and I eagerly set off on the tram to explore Vienna, the City of Music, rich in Baroque architecture and grand monuments. The Austrian capital was everything we had imagined. Elegant horses pull open carriages along wide, tree-lined avenues, and myriad outdoor cafés, palaces, museums and leafy parks draw huge crowds. In the centre of the city stands the majestic St Stephens Cathedral, with immense spires and glazed tiles. We got to the Housdermusik just in time for the free Sunday concerto. It was standing room only for an

Camping - Poland

Countryside - Poland

audience that relished the magic of Mozart and Strauss.

It was surreal that, one day I was riding a tired old motorcycle and battling the elements, and the next I was listening to classical music and playing tourist.

While in Vienna, I found a cheap bulb-horn to replace the non-functioning one on Effie.

I got a call from Australia's SBS Radio. They wanted a phone interview for their Hungarian program. It was great to know that folks back home were following my odyssey.

I spent two days cleaning gear and catching up with paperwork before slipping out at first light and heading northeast on the E462 to Brno in the Czech Republic.

A motorist stopped to chat while I was adjusting the bike. He mentioned that his son was going to a bike rally in Poland on the approaching weekend. It wasn't far out of my way, and, if I could keep Effie going, I thought it would be fun to meet up with other bike enthusiasts. Also, it was refreshing to know that I could now deviate whenever I chose.

Southeast of Brno I stopped, intending to camp on a lovely piece of lawn beside the E462. From there I could take in Napoleon's Hill, scene of his greatest loss in a battle, which took 30,000 lives. Although I felt I was far enough from the nearby truck stop and food outlet to cause no one any trouble, the manager of the McDonalds rolled up and asked me to move on. He must have felt I was lowering the tone of the place. *Bugger, I hadn't even had to time to use the toilet facilities!*

I'd never been a McDonald's regular, but that changed once I began my journey, because it was the one place I could have a wash, shave and anything else I needed to do in scrupulously clean conditions. Then, when I was finished, the girl behind the counter would hand me a bundle of paper napkins to clean the oil off my boots and wipe down Effie's engine once it cooled. All of this for the price of an ice cream cone!

I rarely carry maps, but when a friendly guy presented me with a lovely book of European maps, I could not refuse. From there on, there was no excuse for getting lost again.

I rode on and set up camp 50 kilometres short of Olomouc. Jakub, a young guy who had been following my blog, phoned and asked me to meet him the next evening in the town square of Valasske-Mezirici, 86 kilometres to the northeast. He and his friends took me to his home. There I met his wife Helen, and they put on a great barbeque of sausages, chicken, roast pumpkin, assorted salads, bread and, of course, plenty of beer. What a feast! I'd missed this type of family event more than I'd realised. And, to top it off, Jakub's uncle presented me with a bag of gingerbread made by his wife.

The Czech Republic is famous for its ale, and I probably drank more than I was used to. But, what the heck, it didn't happen often! And I was among friends. With a group of keen motorcyclists looking on, I dismantled the inlet valves to demonstrate how Effie's system worked. Even with a beer or four under my belt, I could still do this job blindfolded.

Next morning, Jakub rode with me to a fuel station, where I got a call from someone called Jiri. I handed the cell phone to Jakub who relayed the message that Jiri's friend in Prague, Libor, had told him to find the 'madman on a motorcycle'. No doubt it was me he had in mind.

Jiri, a vintage motorcycle restorer, suggested we meet at Koprivnice's Museum of Transport, 25 kilometres further north. I bade Jakub farewell and headed off to Koprivnice, where the museum director invited me in to see the collection. And what a collection it was.

Tatra, the renowned Czech vehicle manufacturer, was founded in 1850, under the name Schustala & Company, making wagons and carriages. Then, in 1897 they produced the Präsident, the first motorcar in Eastern Europe. In 1900, they made the first racecar: the Rennzweier. In 1919 — after numerous name changes — the company finally became Tatra, named after the nearby Tatra Mountains. Trucks and tank engines were produced for World War I, then, after the 1938 invasion of Czechoslovakia by Nazi Germany, they continued to produce cars that appealed to the Germans. Tatra's had heavy rear-engines, which did not handle corners well at high speed, resulting in the deaths of scores of German officers. The cars became known as the 'Czech's Secret Weapon' and at one point, German officers were forbidden from driving them.

From 1988–2001, Karel Loprais, the Czech truck racer, won the infamous Dakar rally six times in a Tatra 815 truck, an impressive record by any account.

All the vehicles made by Tatra were on display, including aerodynamic cars from the 1940s, fire trucks, motorised buggies, racing cars and much more. The Museum of Transport, in fact, comprises four separate museums. Unfortunately, I only had time to visit one of them.

When Jiri arrived at the museum, he declared he wanted to ride with me to the Polish border on a more interesting back road route than the hillier, direct one I had planned to take. I only had to pedal a few times along the heavily, tree-lined road, broken at times by quaint villages.

Being towed to Libor's home in the Czech Republic from the Polish border

Polish church

Jiri was going to western Poland to buy motorcycle parts. We stopped for coffee at a roadside café, enjoying the sunshine. Jiri told me how he collected and restored motorcycles for other enthusiasts and when we parted company at the border, he presented me with a limited-edition 10th anniversary medal from his club, the Old Timer Club Helfstyn. I promised I would put it on Effie's tank.

Once in Poland, I called the number I'd been given, only to find the man's father had given me the wrong date for the bike meeting — the Bielsko Biala rally having been held a week earlier.

Through a volunteer interpreter, I was invited to join the man and his family that evening. Armed with an address, I took my bearings and found myself heading along a one-way road, looking in vain for a road going back in the opposite direction. I couldn't find it and, becoming completely lost, gave up. I called my would-be host to explain.

'Oh, that's a pity my friend,' he said, 'My wife baked you a batch of cookies and was looking forward to meeting you.' I apologised, thanked them both, and made camp in a forest just off the road.

Next day, when I headed to Krakow, my bicycle speedo showed that since we left Kathmandu Effie had covered 12,559 kilometres. I had estimated she was good for only about 10,000 kilometres, yet here she was, unbowed and battling on. What a feat! As my Californian friend Jeff would say, 'Yeee-haaa!'

Nervous about pushing her too hard, I frequently willed her on with, 'You can do it, Effie, I know you can!'

Krakow looked to me like just another big city. I stuck to the outskirts where possible, and, once through, hurried on to camp for the night in another forest near Kielce.

For the most part, I'd enjoyed good weather and pleasant scenery. The mornings were chilly enough for thermals, but once the sun came up I had to stop to take them off. The rides through the week had been easy and Effie had coped reasonably well. That was about to change.

33

The Wheels Fall Off

Effie was showing her age. Her rear hub was cracked and many of the holes in the spoke flanges had broken out. My top speed was reduced to 20 kmh, and I had to re-tension the rear spokes every hour. To make matters worse, the pedal gear fell off when I mounted too heavily during a push-start.

I had hoped Effie would make it to Prague, where I could repair the hub at Libor's workshop, but with more than 400 kilometres to go that was unrealistic. I jury-rigged the pedal as best I could by cutting a strip from a coke can and wedging it into the dovetail of the pedal gear to tighten it up. Fifty kilometres from Radomsko, with the light fading fast, I sought refuge in a small village park.

Next morning, disaster struck. The pedal gear fell off again, this time taking the brake rod with it, which then snapped. Now, I had no brakes or foot rests. It was tricky trying to balance the bike with my legs stuck out for the next 20 kilometres. As I searched for an auto repair shop, I kept hoping I wouldn't encounter traffic lights because I had no way of stopping on command.

Luck was with me — until I reached a roundabout. For no apparent reason, a motorist already on the roundabout, stopped directly in front of Effie, possibly out of curiosity, forcing me to take evasive action. As I struggled to keep the bike upright, my leg clipped the vehicle. Had I been a few inches into the roundabout, we surely would have taken a fall. Fortunately, apart from being shaken, I escaped unhurt and no damage was done. The driver, oblivious to the near disaster he had caused, went on his way.

I finally made it into Prezedbortz where Effie and I limped into Auto Centrum Swiech, an auto-spares shop. Tomek, the owner, unable to understand my problems, phoned Tukasc, a schoolteacher, who agreed to come and interpret for us. One of the staff took away the brake rod for welding and the clamp bolt for repair. When I reassembled the bike, everyone looked on in amazement. Tomek refused payment, instead, showering me with gifts of tools, reflective jacket, tyre-repair kit, metallic epoxy, cable ties and hose clamps. I was lost for words.

That wasn't the end of my warm welcome. Tukasc invited me to his home for a shower, after which his mum served me a traditional Polish breakfast. His grandmother, now in her nineties, had a handshake as strong as any I'd ever experienced. Tomek, Tukasc, his mum and grandmother were typical of the kind and generous Polish people I met.

Back on the road, Effie constantly overheated and her engine started up a deep thumping sound. Suspecting a worn main bearing, I pulled into a fuel station to call Jan, Libor's friend in Prague (Libor spoke very little English). I had no Polish phone card and, as I was leaving the country, I asked the cashier if I could use his phone instead. He said his phone had no credit, so I offered to buy some. Forty zlotys, he indicated with his fingers. Ten Euros! That made for a bloody expensive phone call, but I didn't have much choice. I asked Jan if Libor could meet me at the border to take me to his workshop. Effie's days, I feared, were numbered, so the sooner I stripped her down the better. Jan called back to confirm the meeting place, making sure I knew which of the several border crossings was the correct one.

Still with some distance to travel, I had to take it very slowly. Several toll-ways lay ahead and, as always, they proved challenging. Unlike India, where bikes pass through freely, here I had to work out which was the correct lane, then I had to find the right coins to put in the machine. Within minutes, queues formed behind me, some drivers waggling fingers or tooting horns. I apologise now to the many motorists who might have been late for dental appointments, plane flights, court appearances, and family birthday celebrations ... because I was travelling at snail-pace.

Stopping every ten minutes to let the engine rest, it took me the whole day to cover 90 kilometres to the Czech border. Effie laboured, her little engine vibrating so badly I thought she would burst. In my desperation to keep her going, I failed to recognise that Libor had to travel 300 kilometres from Jinocany, southwest of Prague, to meet me. And I had to rely on my rescuer to spot me, because I had no idea who I was looking for as I approached the border.

Then I spotted a car with a trailer going in the opposite direction.

Beautiful Prague - Czech Republic

Outside the Czech Museum - Czech Republic

Fortunately, Libor had seen me, too, and he turned around. We shook hands and loaded Effie on the trailer. Libor has only a few words of English, and we got by with gestures on the long drive to Prague. I was embarrassed that I had dragged him so far from home.

At his workshop, Libor demonstrated how he made film props and other requirements for movie special effects. Like many motorcycle devotees, his car sat outside to make room for the collection of motorcycles in his garage. A true enthusiast, he has immaculate engines and bike paraphernalia displayed throughout his home.

Next day, when I stripped down the engine, my worst fears were confirmed — the main bearing had worn out. I also found the tapered exhaust cam-lobe securing-pin had broken. We fashioned a temporary pin from an old drill shank. Libor put me in touch with an engineer who was able to grind the main bearing of the crankshaft, and another man who could make a bronze main bearing. All this was done in one day, so we were able to finish reassembling most of the engine next morning. Once the motor was back together, I started it up and all seemed okay. Libor's wife, Helena, noticing how skinny I was, made it her mission to feed and care for me. I was among very special people.

Ardie and his wife Josie, avid Dutch motorcyclists who had contacted me via the blog, arranged for us to meet the next weekend, 90 kilometres away at the Bucek camping ground. Ardie said he had a gift for me — a genuine FN seat, one that would be much more comfortable than the one I was using. Effie ran poorly all the way to Bucek, and when I arrived I checked the valve springs and found one had collapsed. I'd not fitted one of the manifold seals correctly. I fixed it, and, to my relief, the engine ran perfectly.

I spent two days relaxing at Bucek, sharing travel adventures with Ardie and Josie. The seat Ardie had brought was an FN original — 100 years old and in sound condition. I borrowed an angle grinder to cut the weld on the original seat adjuster and fit the replacement. I was looking forward to enjoying a wider, more comfortable seat.

Effie ticked along nicely when I returned to Libor's place in Jinocany, and next day Effie and I joined Libor, on his immaculately restored four-cylinder 1924 FN, on a social ride. (Two years before, Libor had toured the Czech Republic on his 1904 Rossler & Jauernig motorcycle, covering a distance of 2,605 kilometres — no mean feat for such an old bike.)

We visited the city of Beroun, finishing the ride at Rokycany after stopping for lunch at a castle and then visiting a hammer mill. Although

Piston problem - Czech Republic

Effie runs again - Czech Republic

Effie had run well, she now had so many broken spokes we decided it would be safer to return to Libor's house in his friend's car and take a trailer to collect my bike next day.

Libor's friend welded the hub and re-drilled the spoke holes. Libor also organised a new set of spokes — and drove 200 kilometres to collect them so that the wheel would be ready next morning for refitting. Nothing ever seemed too much trouble for my friend. It frustrated me that it was impossible to fully show my appreciation.

Libor had also arranged for me to meet Arnost, the curator of the Technical Museum in Prague. Jan, who had a special interest in bicycles, and I enjoyed a conducted tour of the museum. Arnost explained that before reliable carburettors were invented starting a motor required ingesting petrol fumes, with hot water poured into a tube to produce the fumes. In times of need, it seems, it wasn't unusual for the rider to piss in the tube to generate the required fumes.

When I returned to Libor's, and found he had completed the respoking, I decided it was time to fit a new rear tyre and tube. Thanks to the stronger Ensign tyres, I had doubled the distance traveled before having to make a replacement. Though significant rubber remained, it made sense to make the change while the bike was in pieces.

Libor was sure the 21-inch tube could not possibly fit into a 26-inch tyre. Even when I fitted it, I think he still doubted it really worked. Perhaps he didn't understand that the tyre was measured on the outside, and tube on the inside. My friend finished truing the wheel, completing the job a lot faster than I could have. For Libor's generosity and time, as a small token of appreciation, I helped him complete some outdoor furniture he was building.

Soon I was heading into Prague to meet Lynne, who had been in Spain for a week teaching an intensive English program. She was now ensconsed in an Airbnb apartment in the heart of Prague. It was an ideal location for sightseeing, yet, over the next few days, it was also a quiet space to catch up with mail and to relax after walking cobbled streets and laneways.

The night before Lynne and I parted company, we enjoyed a delicious candlelight dinner at the Hotel Residence. In recent weeks, I'd drunk too many beers and sampled way too much local hooch. As I prepared to leave the Czech Republic on the last leg of my journey, I was able to look back with much gratitude for the great friendships I had made. Friends like Jakub and Helen, who had only just welcomed their new daughter; Libor's wife, Helena, who took such good care of me; and of course, Libor, whose assistance had been above and beyond anything I could ever have imagined.

I collected Effie from Libor's house and took the scenic route southwest, through gently rolling hills, towards the German border. When I stopped to take photos of Stahlavy, Mensik, invited me to his restaurant, Moto Pension, for lunch. Mensik brought out plate after plate, until I had to refuse any more. I was beginning to think this was turning into an epicurean tour. Effie, no doubt, groaned under the extra weight.

Later, when I pulled into a fuel station, a motorist walked over and handed me his phone. It was Libor on the line. They had been chatting, and the motorist had mentioned that an old bike had just arrived. Seems Libor has friends everywhere!

After making excellent distance, I camped the night at Babylon, 15 kilometres from the border, ready for an early start. It was an uneventful border crossing into Germany, at Furth im Wald and on to Cham. In the EU, there are no border welcome signs. The tension and drama of my journey had eased since I crossed into Europe, but my excitement was mounting as I drew nearer to my destination.

Effie's performance brought my thoughts back to the job at hand. The engine was vibrating, causing me to stop every 30 kilometres or so to enable it to cool down. Desperate to make it to the FN rally in Bernkastel on September 14, I did my best to keep my speed as low, and the engine as cool, as possible.

Despite my immediate concerns, I was feeling in a celebratory mood, so I splashed out on smoked salmon for dinner. I'd just finished pitching my tent when a passing cyclist suggested I move from the open area I had chosen. Camping wild in Germany was illegal, he said, and 'The police set up their speed cameras here'. I took his advice and moved into nearby trees and out of sight. Around 9.00 pm, two men in army fatigues arrived and insisted I move another 300 metres. They were hunting wild boar, they said, and I was in their line of fire. Maybe camping wild wasn't such a good idea after all!

The pig shooters helped me move my tent out of the firing line. 'It's ironic,' I told them, 'I've been through so many countries considered dangerous, and yet here I find myself a target for sports hunters.' They laughed, promising they would try not to shoot me.

Four beauties - Czech Republic

On a run with Libor - Czech Republic

34

So Close

I imagine, after what happened to me in Iran and Turkey, some might think that I was still taking too many risks. If I'd been on a modern bike, I probably would have sought out camping grounds, but just keeping my ancient machine going was taking all my concentration — everything else seemed far less important.

Effie struggled but managed 170 kilometres the next day. As usual, there were problems, and each time one occurred I'd get nervous. We were so close, yet something could still happen that could bring it all to an end.

To lift power, I tried running the exhaust open by removing the baffle, which was restricting the muffler. This seemed to make a difference, and I got along well until I reached Stuttgart and started looking for my booked accommodation. This meant numerous stops, and push starts, many of them on hills — and most with traffic lights. If I missed the green light, I had to roll back down the hill and try again.

I decided it was easier to park Effie and search on foot. It was 20 degrees, which would normally be perfect riding weather — but not for pushing Effie up hills. I located my Airbnb accommodation, then returned for Effie and parked her in the apartment's garage. After a hot shower and rest, Gudrun, our hostess, kindly drove me to meet Lynne, who arrived by rail from Nuremburg.

There are several Bosch factories in Stuttgart, so I decided to look for quality spark plugs while I was there. The first factory I called on produced only electrical appliances; and when I found Bosch's automotive factory, it was closed for the weekend. I left a message explaining my loose-porcelain problems, wrapped the broken spark plugs in the note, and dropped the lot into the factory's mailbox. I never got a response.

Bernkastel - Germany

Rally breakdown, Bernkastel - Germany

During the planning stage I decided I wanted to ride the Bertha Benz Memorial Parkway. It was on this route through the Black Forest in 1888 that Karl Benz's wife, Bertha, drove her husband's hitherto untested car without his knowledge. The parkway runs between Mannheim and Pforzheim.

There was no petrol in those days — or, for that matter, cars — so Bertha fueled her contraption with alcohol bought from pharmacies. It is also said she used a long hairpin to clean a fuel pipe, and one of her garters to insulate a wire. On her arrival in Pforzheim, she told her husband by telegram of her success. And then a few days later she drove the 100 kilometres back to Mannheim.

Bertha's adventures enabled Karl Benz to make important improvements to his vehicle, including lower gears to tackle hills, and better braking power. I felt it an honour to ride Effie on a route taken by such a forward-looking auto-pioneer. Markers now commemorate Bertha's feat.

I was heading to Bruchsal, in the state of Baden-Wurttemberg, where Daniel, another blog follower, lived. He had invited us to stay at his home when he learned I was riding the Bertha Benz Memorial route. Gudrun drew me a map and took Lynne in her car. However, Gudrun's instructions proved too difficult for me to follow and I ended up lost. I wondered if Bertha had had this much trouble on her ground-breaking drive all those years ago. She certainly wouldn't have had to cope with the heavy traffic I encountered.

Three times I had to stop to refit the number-one inlet spring. It was risky business getting off the road with vehicles tail-gating me. The drivers either wanted a closer look, or were waiting to pass. The inlet-spring problem hadn't cropped up previously and, with me becoming ever more anxious, I found it nerve-wracking.

When we were searching for Daniel's place, Lynne and I were also having trouble trying to stay in touch. I was using a Czech phone card, so couldn't call her. Then her card ran out in mid-conversation. She bought a new card — which didn't work, and this resulted in a long wait in the store to have the problem sorted.

Eventually, when contact was made, it was decided that Lynne should hire a taxi driver to lead her and Gudren to where I was parked. I was only two kilometres away, but it took them an hour to find me, the taxi driver having driven around in circles. Finally, we arrived at Daniel's. I discovered that Daniel, who built motorcycle oil pumps, was restoring a four-cylinder 1913 FN for a friend.

He had organised a meeting with reporters, including a photo shoot, in the centre of town. While I was posing for a picture, the ancient goggles I'd bought in Bulgaria fell off the bike and the lens smashed. I hadn't even had an opportunity to use them, and I knew that replacing the curved glass wouldn't be easy.

Daniel and his wife Nancy gave us the use of their car so that we could tour the region at leisure. We visited the splendid Chateau of Bruchsal, restored after its destruction during World War II. It houses antique mechanical musical instruments, including an organ made for the Titanic that, obviously, missed the boat.

During our stay in Bruchsal, we contacted John, a British expat living nearby. John and I had met the previous year in Castlemaine, Victoria, where we were house-sitting and John and his wife Margaret were visiting. I'd taken the bike out for a trial run that day, and it caught John's eye. A vintage car enthusiast, John became an avid follower of my blog as well as a generous sponsor. It was lovely to catch up and share in the highs and lows of the year past. Spending time with John reminded me of just how small we have made our world.

On September 12, I headed for Bernkastel, where the FN rally was due to take place in a few days. Lynne took the train so she would be there to greet me. It was overcast and chilly when I set out, and never-ending traffic lights were to make it a long day. The rally, known as Treffen in Germany, was expecting many riders from across Europe and Britain. However, Bernkastel wasn't to be the climax of my journey: my ultimate goal was the FN factory in Herstal, in Greater Liege, Belgium, where Effie was made.

The factory in Herstal hadn't made motorcycles since the1960s, but for me it would be nostalgic to be taking Effie back to her roots. Often, on my journey I tried to visualise what it must have been like back in 1910 for a young man to buy a brand new motorcycle and take it out on the rough roads of the day.

He'd be proud no doubt, but pretty nervous, too, considering there were a dozen levers and controls to manage — and always the fear of something going wrong. And he probably would have no idea about what to do should the engine fail. It is likely he had only a basic handbook to assist him. Come to think of it, it all seemed a bit like me as I battled towards Belgium — but I didn't even have a handbook!

I camped in a field surrounded by wind turbines. Light rain fell as I lay in the tent listening to the gentle whoosh of the blades. I was prickling

Bernkastel-Kues - Germany

Belgian club welcome at Bernkastel - Germany

with the excitement of knowing how close I was. So many things could still go wrong over the next several hundred kilometres, but even if I had to push Effie all the way to Herstal, and it took another few months, I was determined we were going to make it.

I guessed it would be my last nights sleep under the stars. If all went well the next day, I'd be toasting my success among a happy crowd of new friends, all motorcycle enthusiasts. I had plenty to celebrate, and I couldn't think of a nicer way of doing it.

35

Sweet Victory

Once the mist cleared, I set off for Bernkastel. A spoke had broken, but I wasn't going to let that stop me. We rode through the narrow streets of picturesque villages and climbed steep mountains. I had to push for more than a kilometre, but even that barely slowed me down.

In the stunning Moselle valley, I passed vineyard-carpeted slopes, and, here and there, rambling castles, some nearly a thousand years old. Barges and cruise boats plied the Mosel.

I was feeling giddy with delight and, as I came out of a long tunnel and saw the charming town of Bernkastel before me, I found myself wanted to cheer loudly. Just one stop at lights, then a left turn onto the bridge and, as Effie and I came over the rise, my heart leapt as I saw Lynne jumping up and down, waving her arms madly. I stopped in the middle of the bridge and, oblivious to the traffic around us, Lynne threw her arms around my neck.

'You made it,' she cheered.

'Effie made it,' I said, choking back tears.

'You made it together. I'm so proud of you, babe, you and Effie. You're both bloody amazing.'

A small crowd gathered: caught up in the excitement yet unaware of how much this moment meant to us. We hugged one another, and exchanged knowing smiles. A warm glow filled my body. I felt invincible after the 14,028 kilometres I'd travelled to reach Bernkastel.

The rally meeting place was only a short distance away, which was just as well. Trying to negotiate roundabouts and traffic lights when I was feeling so lightheaded was tricky. Dieter, the rally organiser, a genial fellow with a huge handlebar moustache, welcomed us enthusiastically and extended an invitation to join his family for supper that evening.

Don't give up yet Effie – Germany

The final stretch – Belgium

From the Hotel Drei Konige balcony, we gazed out across the river, taking in the lush green vineyards and the ruins of Castle Landshut, which overlooks this mediaeval town. I savoured the moment, thinking back to what it had taken to reach this point. All those hills, the pushing, the breakdowns, the physical and mental exhaustion. Somehow, the difficulties seemed to make the triumph even sweeter.

Next day, the sponsor who organised the tyres to be sent to Iran joined us at Bernkastel. I was honoured that Thomas had driven from his home several hundred kilometres away to welcome me to Germany. Unfortunately, he was only able to stay long enough for us all to enjoy a relaxed lunch and a chat before he headed home.

FN riders had begun arriving at rally headquarters and were congratulating me. Effie and I were among people who really understood how gruelling the journey had been for man and machine. It was fascinating to see so many FN models together in one place, and learning the stories behind each.

At times I had to pinch myself that I was commemorating the FN marque and celebrating the culmination of my dream — well, almost! There was still a little way to go.

Sadly, for me, the rally the following day was a disaster. After only 6 kilometres I had to withdraw with mechanical problems. I'd been growing increasingly nervous that I had pushed the little bike too far. It was one thing to have a dream, but another to have unrealistic expectations of a machine of such vintage.

When I first heard that strange noise, I suspected the transmission gears were out of alignment. That would signal a serious problem. Pieter, a local chap, kindly lent me his workshop to remove the rear wheel and engine. The only obvious cause was that the clutch dog was badly worn on one face. The transmission gears, however, were perfect. Whatever it was, I decided it was better to stay out of the rally.

A week later, I was to discover that the noise was only the pedal-gear housing rubbing on the tyre. What a bummer. I missed the run because of a false diagnosis. I was annoyed at myself for panicking. I should have realised Effie wasn't about to give up that close to the finishing line.

Another happy surprise meeting at Bernkastel was with brothers Mark and Geert, who had driven from Holland. With Harry, their dad, they had sponsored my tyres and tubes. Over lunch, we talked bikes, and I showed them a picture of the AJS I'd restored 40 years before.

'I've got a picture of that bike at home,' one of them said. 'I found a calendar in a secondhand bookshop in New Zealand, and your bike was featured in it.' Unbelievably, the picture had been taken nearly 30 years ago.

Another surprise was that a motorcyclist I'd met in Romania had travelled 200 kilometres to congratulate me. I was blown away that so many people were so genuinely interested and would travel this far to give me a pat on the back.

That evening, winemaker Dieter, who had made a splendid job of organising the 10th anniversary event, presented each rally entrant with a bottle of his special vintage, complete with an FN label and cap. Trophies were presented and speeches made. I was proud to accept the 'longest-distance' trophy, and the tears welled up when I expressed my gratitude to all those who had helped me make it that far. The level of interest in Effie was humbling. And it was exhilarating to be part of a fraternity from 10 countries to celebrate this special marque. Many of those present had followed my journey since its inception.

Next day, as I rode out of Bernkastel on the final stage of my journey, Lynne was boarding the train to Liege, taking with her a good deal more luggage than she had when she'd arrived. Bernkastel had added hugely to our store of memories, and I had been swamped with gifts and mementos from many generous friends.

I rode west across Germany to Luxembourg, one of the smallest countries in Europe, and the last before Belgium, Effie's birthplace. I hoped Effie, having come this far, would have enough in reserve to make it across the line. Just to be sure, I decided we'd take our time, and enjoy a leisurely drive through the quiet of the Luxembourg countryside.

It made me smile to see people photographing my GPS (Going Places Slowly) route directions: pieces of paper attached to the fuel tank for easy reading. They worked well for me, and certainly beat endless folding and unfolding of maps.

Not everything though was going according to plan. Oil and grease inside the pedal gear cone in the hub made it impossible to assist Effie by pedalling. So it meant a lot of pushing up each hill. And there were plenty of those. If I'd thought of it earlier, WD40 would have fixed the problem.

Still, I made good time, arriving in the Belgian municipality of Gouvy, on the northern border of Luxembourg, a day earlier than planned.

Next day, once the fog lifted, Bruno, a fellow motorcyclist, and I set off to wend our way towards Marche-En-Famenne, via Bastogne, stopping at his dad's workshop, so that he, too, could inspect Effie.

Pascal, another vintage bike enthusiast, joined us at Bastogne and we posed at the Battle of the Bulge monument for photographs on our three Belgian marques — a Gillet, a Sarolea and an FN. Then it was a leisurely ride on to Marche-En-Famenne to spend the evening with members of Moto Retro Famene Ardenne, hosted by Claude and Pierrette.

As expected, my journey was an object of media interest in Effie's homeland. After a local newspaper reporter and one from a motorcycle magazine interviewed me, I was presented with a replica FN plaque and a sculpture of a gentleman in period costume standing beside an FN, both masterfully created by club members. The inscription on the sculpture read, 'Thank you for making us dream.'

I was lost for words. These unique gifts reminded me that so many people had participated in my adventure. And the reward of accomplishment was not for me alone — it was for everyone. The moment seemed fitting to share a nice thought by Oliver Wendell Holmes: 'Men do not stop playing because they grow old. They grow old because they stop playing.'

Next morning, Claude and Pierre, who had ridden from Liege, joined me for the last leg of my odyssey.

I took several deep breaths!

This is it.

The end is in sight!

Along the way, we met up with Michel on his original Bovy motorcycle. We visited a school where the children, intrigued by our magnificent old machines, asked the usual questions — this time in French.

It was an easy ride on to Liege. We had to stop once for Effie to cool down. And the brake pawl had worn out again. Fortunately, when we stopped further on to take a tour of the Public Transport Museum in the Vennes-Fetinne district of Liege, I was able to leave the pawl for welding in the capable hands of an engineer.

Housed in a former tramway depot, the museum has a collection of vehicles and memorabilia ranging from the 18th century to the present day. Beautifully restored carriages, trams and trolleybuses transported us back to bygone eras.

All the time, I was feeling distracted. Trying to remain calm, I had to close my eyes now and then and take a deep breath. It felt as if time had come to a standstill. So close was I to my destination, I felt I could practically smell it. After lunch, while the repairs were being done, the brake was reassembled, and we were able to set off for Herstal.

As we drew closer to our destination, flashbacks of the past eight months tumbled through my mind: the hardships, the numbing exhaustion, constant discomfort, times when I really thought I wasn't going to make it ... I was on the cusp of what I had looked forward to for so long — to be riding Effie up to the entrance of the factory where her life had begun more than a century before.

I passed the brownstone terraced houses, whose appearance probably had changed little over the years. It all seemed unreal. *Is this how Alice felt when she fell down the rabbit hole?* My insides quivered like a hummingbird on a hibiscus. There they were, the huge steel gates, only metres away. I looked back at my companions. I was grinning like the Cheshire cat. Effie and I had arrived — we had finally bloody well arrived!

36

Back to Where it all Began

We'd made it! As I drew up at the gates of the Herstal Group factory, Lynne was behind the camera trying to capture the moment. She and Pierre's wife, Martine, had been waiting for hours, sometimes wondering if we were ever going to arrive.

I took off my helmet. Light rain touched my face as I looked up and whispered, 'Thank you', to no one in particular. Lynne sprinted over and threw her arms around my neck.

'Congratulations, Ronnie, you got to live your dream,' she cried, her eyes glistening, 'I never doubted you would.'

I should have been jumping for joy, but I doubt I had it in me. Instead, I had goosebumps, and felt giddy with relief. Congratulations showered on me from motorcycle friends and factory workers crowding around. I posed for cameras in front of the impressive FN logo and factory. Lynne captured Effie's bicycle speedometer — 14,606 kilometres. Some distance!

Robert Sauvage, CEO of the Ars Mechanica Foundation, joined us. A keen motorcyclist himself, he shook my hand warmly and invited us to return for a formal reception two days later. I hadn't expected any recognition, but it was gratifying to know that he and others in the field truly appreciated what an epic ride I had made; a journey that had taken stamina and endurance, both of which, at times, I hadn't always been sure I had in me.

On Friday morning, after a late start — due to me not setting my clock to local time — we set off in a group of about 20 motorcycles, heading for Herstal. Just before we arrived at the factory, the other riders pulled aside and waved me into the lead. With mixed emotions, I passed through the gates of FN Herstal. It was Friday, September 21, 2012 — 33 weeks after I had left Australia — and I was a formal guest of the company that

Final speedo reading - Belgium

Effie did it!

had made Effie 102 years before and shipped her to New Zealand. It was with intense pride that I considered what Effie and I had accomplished together in the name of FN. That our journey was now over filled me with a mixture of relief, excitement and the crazy idea that our journey hadn't been so bad after all!

I was overwhelmed by the sincere enthusiasm and genuine support from everyone — members of veteran motorcycle clubs, other motorcycle enthusiasts, and the FN management and workers. Unfortunately, Lynne was unwell and wasn't there to help me celebrate. But I knew she was with me in spirit.

And what a celebration it was. The Australian flag flew in honour of the occasion, many toasts were made, and I was showered with presents, including a special medallion and a centennial anniversary trophy. The efforts of those who made the event possible were much appreciated even though I would have settled for much less fuss.

It was a perfect time to remember all those I'd met along the way. And it had always been a thrill to know my adventures were being shared with hundreds of people around the world via my blog. Their comments and support had been a great source of encouragement.

After the luncheon, I enjoyed a guided tour of the showroom, and had the opportunity to see restored FN cars and motorcycles in the company collection, and I learnt a lot about what the company had done after it ceased motorcycle production in 1965.

The celebrations over, I rode back into Liege and we spent a few days with Pierre and Martine. At the local Veteran Moto Club Belge meeting, I shared pictures of my travels and was particularly touched when the Australian anthem was played during the evening. I could only hope that, one day, my Belgian friends would visit Australia and I could repay their hospitality.

It felt a little strange, and somewhat disconcerting, not to be spinning Effie's back wheel each day, jumping on and coaxing her along. I would miss the songs I sang to keep my spirits up, the sound of her little engine valiantly chugging on and defying the incredible challenges she faced.

Lynne too, had enjoyed her own adventure, especially through countries that usually receive a bad rap in the West. Striking up conversations with strangers came easy to her. She haggled over prices and, like me, was game to try anything. Even having her head covered in public had not been as bad as she had imagined. Hauling luggage up and down stairs, on trains, and over cobblestones was probably Lynne's greatest challenge, because her knees were in such bad shape. If not for the added weight of tubes and spare parts she was carrying for me, a backpack may have sufficed. Despite this, she had no regrets, and had come away with many happy memories.

We were reminded of how years before — a friend, who had never travelled outside the USA — arranged to meet us in Mexico City. Her dentist warned her on the day before her departure, not to go. It was dangerous, he said. This was a man who had never crossed the border. Our friend cancelled her ticket, missing out on, what proved to be for us, one of the highlights of South America. We've always figured that most things are worth trying at least once … even riding an antiquated motorcycle across the world!

Before we headed back down under, we took the opportunity to see more of Europe and to meet up again with friends, including Harry and Nel De Boer, Nick, Freddy and Jacques who had been some of our keenest supporters. Jacques Maertens had supplied information, photos and diagrams during the restoration and he presented me with a reproduction set of pedals for Effie. They suited her admirably.

Harry learned that a post-vintage Zundapp and sidecar were waiting to be shipped from the Netherlands to Sydney. Hans, the buyer, generously agreed that Effie could share a pallet with his latest acquisition. With the help of Dutch Lion Motorcycles, Effie was loaded alongside the Zundapp and wrapped in plastic. It would be many months before she would arrive, safely, back in Australia. Robert Sauvage, FN CEO, had kindly offered to ship everything we had accumulated in recent weeks, back to Australia. That was a huge relief.

Life would soon return to normal. Our house in Bali had sold. This meant that, in a few weeks, we would be able to pack up and ship our belongings from Bali to Tasmania, where we planned to settle.

Now it was time to take the fast train to Germany for our flight back to Australia. Christine and Philippe, our Airbnb hosts in Liege, had become close friends and it had been hard to say goodbye to this delightful couple.

As the scenery flashed by, I remembered back to the presentation outside the FN plant when the CEO asked, 'What was the purpose of your journey?'

'I am here to settle a warranty issue,' I said tongue-in-cheek.

'Unfortunately,' Robert replied, 'the warranty period only applied for the first 100 years.'

A resounding cheer echoed from the crowd.

Ron arrives at FN factory - Belgium

With the FN CEO - Herstal, Belgium

Postscript

I set out on this solo journey optimistic that I could do it on my own. But I soon learned none of us are ever truly alone. There are family, friends, and strangers who believe in us: who provide support, comfort and love when we need it most. I thank each and every person who contributed to making my adventure more fulfilling.

Effie may not have been built with such a torturous odyssey in mind but I take my hat off to her and those innovative FN pioneers who had the foresight to design this marvel of engineering. With a supreme effort on Effie's part, my mechanical skills and a little ingenuity we worked as a team.

It had been an incredible adventure and yet still I am often asked, 'But isn't it dangerous to go to those countries?'

Yes, there are dangerous places with crazy people in every corner of the world, but I believe there's probably more chance of being struck by a tram than meeting a suicide bomber. I have found most people are just like me with the same dreams and desires. Keeping this in mind helps put it all into perspective. There were definitely times when I could have willingly chucked in towel. But accepting that nothing worth doing is ever easy definitely made the victory sweeter.

Before I left Belgium I arranged for my sleeping bag and camping gear to be given to a homeless person. Hopefully it would offer some comfort and perhaps even a little of my good fortune would rub off on the recipient.

Effie arrived back in Australia by sea after a long and much anticipated wait. A slight hiccup occurred when the Australian customs agent insisted the carnet needed to be stamped in the country of departure. I had tried in Germany — for this very reason — to find a customs office to get a stamp, but as carnets are not required for Europe, no one had a stamp! Fortunately the motoring organisation that issued the carnet accepted my explanation without question and refunded my guarantee deposit.

Effie made it to Tasmania by road transport and was kept in storage until our new home was completed in December 2013.

With a new workshop and tools on hand I was able to begin the process of stripping the motorcycle down to replace any worn parts. The bike's exterior will remain relatively unrestored to honour her incredible feat. The one concession though will be to give Effie a gearbox to make it easier on the hills, and thanks to Dave, a fellow Tasmanian vintagent, she's to sport a snazzy wicker sidecar so Lynne can accompany us on our next adventure.

I plan on returning to Europe to take part in a few veteran motorcycle events, and last, but not least, to ride coast to coast across the USA. A tall order I know, but I'm confident that once the restoration is complete Effie will be as good as new and able to rise to the occasion.

My journey was a test of endurance for man and machine. And I admit it's not a challenge that would suit everyone. Despite experiencing several close calls, I rarely felt unsafe. Luck, karma, call it what you will, does, I believe, play a large part in any bold undertaking. For me, it isn't dying that is scary. It's doing nothing.

I love the saying by E. James Rohn, 'If you are not willing to risk the unusual, you will have to settle for the ordinary.'

Some Facts & figures

- 1910 FN (Fabrique Nationale) four cylinder in-line engine
- Capacity 498cc
- Automatic inlet valve & camshaft driven exhaust
- Shaft drive with clutch
- Magneto ignition
- 26×2.5 beaded edge tyres
- Fuel capacity 6 litres
- Oil capacity 2 litres
- Oil system total loss via dripper
- Brakes on rear wheel only
- Modified aluminum pistons
- Pedal start

- Total distance covered   14606 kilometres
- Countries ridden through   15
- Petrol used   726 litres
- Oil used   24.6 litres
- Tyres replaced   3 rear tyres
- Spark plugs replaced   3 sets x 4
- Inlet valve springs replaced   20
- Spokes broken   120

- Fuel consumption on the journey was approximately 20 kms to the litre
- Grease was used as the lubrication for all parts of the transmission
- The rear wheel has a double braking system, consisting of an internal expanding band brake and an externally contracting drum brake.
- I modified a large ring spanner to make a five-spanner tool kit to fit every nut on the bike. A spark plug operated tyre pump reduced the need for a conventional hand pump and was a lot easier to use as the piston of the engine inflated the tube.

What I Carried

- 2 x 5-litre cans of spare fuel, container of spare oil
- 2 x 21-inch spare tubes, 3 spare tyres, puncture repair kit
- Tyre gauge, set bicycle tyre levers
- Sparkplug tyre pump, 4 spare spark plugs
- 2 spare pistons, piston rings
- 4 exhaust valve springs, 1 exhaust valve, 1 inlet valve, 50 inlet valve springs
- 2 spare sets front wheel bearings, carburettor jets
- 3 carbon magneto brushes, magneto spanners, feeler gauges
- Flat file, multi-purpose spanner, 4 inch shifting spanner, 5/8 ring open-ender
- 12/13 open ender spanner, spoke key, 3 screwdrivers
- 6 spare sight-glass plastic windows, bundle of cable ties
- Sealants, grease, gasket paper, assorted washers, nuts and bolts

Multipurpose tool

- Backpack, 2 Dry Rider soft panniers, 2 waterproof stuff bags, 4 bungie-cords
- Daniese Waterproof Boots, 1 pair sandals
- 2 helmets & goggles, reflective vest
- Gloves, scarf, one fleece sweater
- Rain poncho, Huskie Jacket, wet weather pants, 1 pair cargo pants
- 2 T-shirts, 2 long-sleeved shirts, 1 pair shorts
- 2 pair briefs, thermal underwear
- 1 pair thermal socks, 1 pair woollen socks
- 1 x two man dome tent weighing 3 kg, Thermarest ground mattress
- Sleeping bag & silk liner
- Towel, shaving gear, soap, toothpaste & toilet paper
- Stainless cup, knife, fork spoon set, 2 folding plates (bowl & plate)
- Water bottle, whistle, headlamp, small torch
- First aid kit, 1 pair reading glasses
- Solar charger, combination lock
- Mobile phone, camera, chargers, SIM cards
- Passport, carnet, maps, credit cards & cash
- Health & third party insurance, international driver's license

Costs

Airfares, freight, visas,
clothing & camping gear,
spares, petrol, oil,
accommodation & daily expenses

Total trip: approx $20,000

Thanks to all the true believers

Printed in April 2022
by Rotomail Italia S.p.A., Vignate (MI) - Italy